DYNAMICS
OF STILLNESS

Ian Wright

BSc (OST) DPO. FSCCO. MOCI.

I dedicate this book to my greatest teachers over the years — my patients of all ages who have taught me so much about overcoming the overwhelming difficulties of coping with anxiety. Thank you.

CONTENTS

ACKNOWLEDGEMENTS

I owe a huge debt of gratitude to my teachers over the last 30 years. The Osteopaths both living and passed include Dr Andrew Taylor Still, Dr Will Sutherland, Dr Edna Lay, Dr Anne Wales, Dr Rollin Becker, Stuart Korth and Dr Jim Jealous.

My greatest teachers though are my patients, especially those special children, who never fail to amaze me. Each day I learn a little more and deepen my understanding and love of life through my practice.

This book has been influenced by a lifetime of study of Taoism, especially the works of the 'Complete Reality Schools' to which I am greatly indebted. There are also threads within this work influenced by various schools of Buddhism. Other threads of influence come from the works of Johann Wolfgang von Goethe and the spiritual practices of Rudolf Steiner.

The nature connection of some of the indigenous world tribes have strongly influenced my practice, including the Bushmen of the Kalahari through the works of Laurens Van de Post, and the Guatamalan Mayans who I had the good fortune to live with and learn from for 6 months in the late 1990's.

To my great friend and colleague Mary Bollingbroke - we learnt how to sense the natural world together, both within our patients and the world around us.

To my wonderful three children Lou, Mia and Dylan, who continue daily to open my heart with love.

Lastly, to my wife Mara- my partner, my life.

Ian Wright

Bsc(ost) DPO. FSCCO. MOCI.

ABOUT THE AUTHOR

 Ian Wright studied Osteopathy at the British School of Osteopathy in 1988-1992. He was taught by two psychoanalysts who were both osteopaths and became fascinated by the interaction between the mind and the body, which led him on a journey of discovery.

Ian has been studying meditation practices for over thirty years, especially Buddhist and Taoist practices, and has been teaching Osteopathy and Paediatrics for over thirty years all over the world, including in the UK, Ireland, Russia, Germany, Italy, Sweden, Spain and Australia.

In 2009, Ian started the Daisy Clinic in Ireland, a charity Paediatric Clinic with the combined function of treating children with complex special needs and teaching graduate Osteopaths a postgraduate diploma in Paediatrics.

He started teaching Dynamics of Stillness courses in 2010. On these courses, participants learn a series of meditations, contemplations and advanced sensory practices to help them find a deep sense of Neutral in themselves, reconnect with nature and reconnect with their own potential for health.

Dynamics of Stillness by Ian Wright was published October 2019 by Eddison Books London.

Ian has reached out to many people via hundreds of podcasts, especially in the realms of self-care, managing anxiety and meditation practice; these are available at Dynamicsofstillness.com

Ian has been working with people of all ages suffering with anxiety for over thirty years; he practises in Ireland, London and Italy.

Introduction

This book is offering something genuinely new and different. It is based on a course I have been teaching for over ten years. It is different from a normal meditation practice in that meditation is not the [main] purpose of what we are doing.

This course is based on thirty-six practices. These involve techniques for developing our sensory awareness whilst at the same time [establishing] a very deep connection to Stillness and the gentle Fluid Tides, in nature and within us. The course takes us step-by-step into an ever-deepening practice. This process helps us become aware of how we use our senses. It seeks to re-pattern our senses to work towards developing a Holistic Felt-Sense - the ability to feel and sense wholeness within ourselves and nature.

Along the journey, we learn some very special techniques to connect us to the Great Fluid Tides in nature. These techniques help us to understand indigenous peoples' practices and the *Story on the Wind*. We explore a wide variety of ideas and practices, from those of advanced Daoist wizards from more than a millennium ago, to the most advanced [ideas in] modern physics, cell biology and fluid dynamics. We work on connecting these elements, but most importantly we learn to sense them within ourselves, in nature and in others.

We learn an important lesson in shifting our attention and awareness from blocks and uneasiness in our body to the potential for true Health. From this, we learn techniques for self-healing and for healing others.

As we progress with each practice, we deepen our self-acceptance into the idea of Soul Works. At the same time, we learn to let our attention be moved by the moment to a proliferating Stillness and, eventually, to a Dynamic Stillness.

At the end of each chapter is a practice. You can either read through the practice or download it and listen to me as I take you through each of them step-by-step until, finally, we have no need for techniques or steps.

I wish you well and hope you really enjoy these practices.

Chapter 1

Finding Our Neutral

It is amazing how much chatter goes on in our brains! Every waking second, we are processing information, making decisions and thinking. From the moment we wake up we are thinking about something: what am I doing today, what shall I wear, what shall I eat? Alongside all these day-to-day simple thoughts we have, there are undercurrents of deeper murmurings: why am I unhappy, is this job right, am I in the right relationship, is my child really ok at school, why do I look this way? Different aspects of ourselves vie for attention, our ego talks to us, perhaps saying 'I really deserve better'. Our emotions raise their heads in subtle ways through grief, fear, anger and guilt.

With all these thoughts going on at the same time, it is amazing how we function at all! Our only respite is when we are listening to music, watching TV, talking, or some other form of sensory excitement. These activities can be relaxing, connecting, calming and even meditative, but

3

they can also be a distraction from our lives. This world of information overload bombards us. Advertising, for example, can be designed to appeal to our ego and to our emotional vulnerabilities. It can be designed to trigger an emotional response in us, for example saying if you eat this, or do this, you will have the perfect body and be happy. This also implies that we cannot be happy without the product that the advertiser is pushing us to buy.

One consequence of this information overload is that we can feel unhappy, empty and confused. We then find that we need to develop strategies for coping with these uncomfortable feelings. Some strategies lead to more unhealthy feelings and physical sensations. However, it is also possible to choose to seek out healthier patterns of behaviour to satisfy our deeper selves.

Sleep should provide us with rest and relaxation. But with our senses being overstimulated, our sleep is often disturbed. Our nervous systems find it hard to wind down enough to get to sleep. When our nervous systems do not get the chance to settle into a quiet place, how could we fall into a natural sleep? And even if we do we can awaken soon after, thinking and worrying again.

The modern problems associated with getting good quality sleep have meant that overcoming sleep issues has become a multi-billion-pound industry. There are hundreds of apps for sale, offering sleep meditations, music and electronic signals that are said to calm the brain. There are zero gravity beds, that is, with foam and air in the mattress and sleeping like an astronaut, at a 60º angle to optimize blood flow. There are thermostatic beds, designed to keep us at a constant 15ºC (supposedly the optimum sleep temperature). In the future, I predict that we may have very complex technologies to help us get to and maintain sleep.

But maybe we need to address the underlying issues with sleep difficulties and find a method which, when practiced daily, can change improve this dynamic and start to offer a sense of peace, tranquility and connection.

There are age-old techniques that are designed to help us improve the quality of our lives, including prayer, meditation, yoga and taking exercise. But how often do we enter these with a quiet mind? Through these techniques, we may occasionally we find a moment's peace – thankfully – but we usually still bring along the chatter! Our thinking mind comes in and says: 'am I meditating right? I only have 7 minutes left before waking up the kids for school, and little Johnny needs to bring his violin today!' Before we can potentially enter this world of stillness, peace and inspiration, we need to find the right place to start. We need to learn to be able to take our minds out of gear, to find our Neutral.

Our Neutral is a place that can be likened to taking the car out of gear. Our minds tend to be driving us ever onwards, to the next destination, thinking, thinking, always driving and striving onwards. In Neutral our mind relaxes its grip, albeit temporarily. We take it out of gear and we start to relax. This relaxation provides the groundwork for deeper practices to flourish.

It is interesting to note that children are often in this neutral state naturally. It is a beautiful natural state where they are in the moment and free to act spontaneously and without judgment. They seem to be undistracted and they can act and react in the moment, free of consideration for anything but themselves and their current experiences.

This state of being in neutral tends to slowly diminish as we enter our early teens: the hormones kick in; social pressure mounts and our internal judge starts to appear. At the same time as we start to become self-aware, this natural state of being starts to wane. During this time, when we begin to compare ourselves to our peer group and to media figures - where we never feel quite good enough and we have the sense of needing to find our place in the world - we set a certain tone in our nervous systems and the natural spontaneous neutral seems to slowly go. As we grow from childhood to adulthood, our reasoning capabilities become more dominant a requirement to satisfy social norms. As such, it seems that the more we use our brains to reason, the less we can find a quiet, neutral way of being.

Incidentally, in my work as an osteopath, I have noticed that this crossover point – where we lose our spontaneity in favour of reasoning - seems to be happening younger and younger. We are now starting to see it in our eight-year olds. Many younger children are subject to overt social pressures from many sources, including TV and social media, particularly advertising. This is a problem. I see too many young children - from happy homes, where school is fine - suffering from typical symptoms of stress: headaches, tummy aches, digestive problems and the inability to sleep effectively. Twenty years ago, it would be only occasionally that a child so young would be suffering from these generalized stress-related symptoms, unless there was a strong reason for it.

Today, it is much more common. With all these external social pressures affecting them - and living in a world where they have this constant stimulation of their senses - it seems that it has become harder than ever for our children to be in a natural state of neutral.

When we are in a state of neutral, it seems to have an interesting effect on our nervous systems. There are various parts of our nervous systems, which can become irritated, when in a state of high alert. The autonomic nervous system - that is, the automatic body systems, such as our breathing, our heart beating and our digestive processes in the body - has two parts: the *sympathetic* and *parasympathetic* nervous systems.

The sympathetic system raises our heartbeat, blood pressure and constricts our blood vessels. The parasympathetic system lowers or slows down these systems. These two systems work in harmony with one another, with opposing effects. The sympathetic element deals with an excitatory phase − the so-called *flight/fright/fight response*. When an emergency arises, we respond from a survival level instinct in one of three ways − to stand and fight, to take flight and run away or to freeze in fear. This process uses a quick and large release of adrenaline in response to an emergency or perceived emergency. This release puts a great deal of strain on our nervous systems and can only be sustained for a very short time. Modern lifestyles simulate excessively activate and overstimulate this process. Parasympathetic response comes in to redress this imbalance and harmonise the body's systems.

One effect of this type of excitation is that adrenal glands which sit on top of both our kidneys become stimulated and pump out adrenaline. You know that feeling when you are in a state of nervous excitement, from fear or great anticipation or nervousness? It feels like a buzzing in our brain and throughout our body. Our nerves become super-reactive, our heart rate and blood pressure rise. We may also have sweaty palms and our pupils will constrict. By doing this we are preparing our bodies for the flight/fright/fight response created by the sympathetic nervous system when our bodies will go into superdrive and ready for the perceived showdown.

This reaction should arise only very occasionally. In the modern world of overstimulation and super-stress, our bodies are in this state far too often, albeit in a subtle way. This sense of overdrive is further sustained by stimulants we are drawn to, especially coffee and alcohol, which can stimulate the adrenal glands directly and maintain this level of readiness. This keeps our bodies in a low-level state of anxiety too much of the time.

Over time, this has a direct effect on several of our body systems. This heightened state of stimulation can also lead to an increase in our pulse rates and blood pressure and it can constrict our capillary beds. The effect of this is to decrease the blood supply to our organs and body and put a strain on our cardiovascular systems. One very common example of excessive adrenal stress is the tightening of the sphincters in our bowels, thereby slowing down the movement of the food inside. This can lead to physical health problems, including constipation and diarrhoea.

This adrenal overstimulation is what directly affects our ability to sleep. We need our brains to be in neutral to sleep and adrenaline prevents this. You remember those times when you had something important to do next day or were worrying about something? It is so hard to switch off and get to sleep. Again, we are reminded of the natural ability of children who usually find it so easy to get to sleep - wherever we lay our heads at the end of a tiring, active day. As we get older that simple switch-off process becomes harder. We tend to wind down slowly over a few hours and wait until we are almost dropping off to try to sleep. Or we take to medications or alcohol to help us relax. Actively taking our brains out of gear could significantly help our ability both to get to sleep and to improve our sleep quality. That can only be a good thing!

Let's start to see if we can take our nervous systems out of gear and see if we can find some degree of neutral. This neutral state is a vital pre-requisite for all later techniques.

CONTEMPLATION 1

Finding Our Quiet Neutral

First, we need to work out when, where and how to practice:

You can be sitting in nature, lying in bed, riding a train or a plane or even walking or running. But to start with let's try this sitting comfortably in a chair, feet on the ground, spine quite straight but not tense. Feel the bones of your bottom on the chair, allow yourself to feel the weight of your body on the chair.

Let your head be upright but let go of any tension in the neck, just let it soften in your mind, let your chest have the sense of being wide, let your eyes relax, feel the eyeball soften, let your hands sit comfortably in your lap.

Keep your eyes open but let your vision be nonspecific just relaxed, or - if this is hard - gently close them. Now just let go of your awareness.

- Become aware of chatter:

The first thing is to realize that there is all this chatter going on and to wake up to that. An age-old Buddhist technique for effective meditation is to become aware of the noise in our head but to do nothing about it, to become like an impartial observer of it, adding a healthy sprinkle of compassion for ourselves: not to judge it, or try to control or stop it in any way. Awareness is a huge step for us - to observe this chatter with no judgment.

- Maintain awareness of the quiet behind the chatter:

  Here let us do something important, namely not to try to stop the noise. We must actively allow it, let our minds wander into the past, the future, thoughts, ideas, places, people, worries, fears, anticipations, whatever - but we must also do something very important which is to maintain awareness of the quiet behind the chatter.

There are many techniques to achieve this. My favourite technique, which you can do on in loud environments even on the metro or in a meeting. It is also excellent if you are finding it difficult to get to sleep:

- *Let's bring our attention gently onto our breathing, but let's notice something delicate and soft in our breathing. This is not deep breathing, it is quite shallow breathing. As soon as we turn our awareness to this delicacy in the breath the usual response from our body/mind is for a million thoughts to demand our attention. Now let's really allow these thoughts, never suppress them, but all the while let's bring our*

11

attention back to the softness in our breathing. Even if we are in great pain, we can try to treat the pain like noise and allow the feeling of the pain. All the while, keep bringing our attention back to something that feels soft or gentle in our breathing.

I have taught this to hundreds of children and adults and it has been a very helpful practice to develop. It is hard to do at the beginning, but with a little practice you can start to maintain this for a few minutes. If you can do this, you tend to find a sense of quietness comes in. Often people report a warm feeling in their chest and they start to gain the feeling of some peace.

Now don't try to hold on to any warm or peaceful feeling, just quietly observe it coming and going. Maintain your concentration on the delicacy in your breathing, the quiet sweet softness of your breath. Just do this for 3-4 minutes at first then return to it later. The ability to concentrate on this softness builds as we practice. Our sense of neutral is when our brain switches down a gear, just for a minute or two at the beginning. It will become easier and quieter with practice. If stressed this is harder to do but, if you are persistent, it can calm down those feelings of stress and anxiety.

Practice this technique as much as you can but, ideally, at least once or twice a day.

The technique is simple, but it is very effective. It not only starts to bring us to our neutral point, it also refocuses our attention from feeling what is wrong in our bodies, to what feels well, gentle and delicate - an expression of our Health - which is a huge step.

Over a period of days and weeks you will retrain your mind/body into starting to feel neutral. This can bring peace and you can even start to find yourself slipping into neutral naturally without trying.

This is only the beginning! We will build many layers of technique from here. Each stage is vital in the practice.

Conclusion

So far, we have just introduced the idea of bringing a little quiet neutral to our racing minds and senses. This is the beginning of our practice. Keep trying this technique even if you find it hard at first. The secret is to completely accept any feeling or sensation which arises in you, even if that feeling is one of being deeply anxious - it's ok, let it be. From this point, we will start to develop our practice in the coming chapters.

Chapter 2

Accepting, Allowing and

Observing

We have started on the path to develop a practice which if we can just work a little on daily - even for 10 minutes - I hope will soon start to bring real palpable benefits. These benefits will come in our sense of neutral, peace, our ability to cope with stress, and our deepening connection to the fields and natural tides in our body, and nature as a whole.

In the first contemplation, we started to bring our awareness to the noise, internally and externally, and started to actively bring our awareness to the softness in our breathing. But usually, as soon as we start this process - as soon as we sit down and start to quieten our minds to look towards finding a degree of Neutral - we are bombarded with a whole plethora of thoughts, feelings and sensations.

Thoughts are the usual story, like our worries: what's for dinner, I must pay that bill, etc. Feelings are slightly deeper and can be sadness, happiness [or perhaps] anger. Sensations are feelings in our body - comfort or, more often, discomfort. They can also be little aches and pains and niggles that we all have. This is entirely *normal*. It happens to everyone, even seasoned meditators and teachers.

There is a way to move past these feelings, thoughts and sensations. Our normal response is to try to push them away, try to judge them or react to them, especially emotions. The way through this, to change this response, is to do the opposite, to *not react* - to accept, allow and eventually just observe these thoughts, feelings and sensations.

If we realize that these thoughts and sensations are *impermanent* - meaning that they come, and they go - we just must wait, and they will pass, like clouds across a clear blue sky.

What happens for us is that a thought, or a movement of the mind or body occurs, and we react to it. From that reaction, we continue with a sequence of reactions. These reactions can go on and as we continue to react, our minds get cloudy and agitated. This is life!

The amazing trick here is if we learn *not* to react to these thoughts or sensations or feelings, the sequence of reactions will gradually slow down and even stop, and our mental *sky* can become clear and crystalline blue.

So, how do we stop these reactions of the mind?

Accept

The first step is to *ACCEPT* that you and everyone in the world has thoughts feelings, and sensations - it is part of being alive and human. Accepting this fact gives us a little break from our eternal self-judgement. We can be so hard on ourselves, especially when trying to sit and find a little peace in ourselves. If we, by just trying to accept this – that it is okay to have thoughts and sensations - it gives us a little window of self-acceptance to build on.

Allow

The second step on this path is to *ALLOW* these sensations and thoughts to arise - let them come. The very action of *allowing* changes our dynamic to them, it has an effect of softening them, as opposed to reacting to them, which seems to act to harden them. What tends to happen here is that the more we allow, the deeper the thoughts, emotions and sensations are that arise. It is as if the mind is saying "Hey! Listen to me!"

So just *keep allowing* these thoughts, sensations, emotions and thoughts to arise. The sensations can be anything from 'my leg is sore' to 'I'm hungry' to 'I forgot I had to pay that bill today', on and on to deeper feelings of sadness and old grief. Whatever it is, just allow it, but do not indulge it: let the feeling, emotion or sensation come.

What is amazing is that even deep pain and grief, if it comes up and you FULLY allow it – without any reaction to it – even the strongest emotion will soften and start to pass. Even that deep emotion is impermanent. Do not let your mind attach and react to it. Just let it come, allow it and it will soften and start to pass. It can be helpful to see these sensations as clouds across a perfect blue sky, gently but continually moving in and out of your awareness.

Observe

From this important standpoint of ACCEPTING and ALLOWING you will gradually come to a point of just OBSERVING these thoughts and sensations, of becoming totally impartial to them without indulging or reacting.

This change of approach takes time and practice. I have been applying this practice for over twenty years and I still get caught out! The point is, if we allow and accept the fact that we will never perfect this, that we can only gradually get better at it, it gives our little internal judge the day off!

It's good to start applying these techniques whenever you become present to your thoughts, sensations and emotions, whether you are sitting down to practice these exercises, in front of your angry boss or with an irritable child.

This process of accepting and allowing will become incredibly freeing, and if practiced daily can become a part of your interaction with life, which may, itself alone, bring peace.

In my work as an osteopath, I spend much of my day working with children and tiny babies. Often the babies are extremely irritable, with colic or reflux for example, and they are in distress. What I do is as soon as I approach them is I apply these three techniques - that of accepting, allowing and observing. This means that my body starts to relax and this in turn can help the baby relax. It is a simple, but very effective technique to apply to many different situations.

Buddhists talk of our humanely suffering as impermanent and have a variety of methods to overcome these thoughts, feelings and emotions. Some practices will encourage the practitioner to say, "thinking, thinking" when these thoughts, feelings and emotions come up.

Others look at focusing on differing aspects of the breath.

For me just the process of accepting, allowing and observing gives me the opportunity to encourage a deeper process within myself.

Let's try to put this into practice.

CONTEMPLATION 2

Accepting, Allowing and Observing

Let's find a quiet, comfortable spot to spend a few minutes.

Get comfortable and allow yourself to feel your back against the chair and your bottom on the seat. Just enjoy the sensation of your weight being held up by the chair.

Now sit quietly and bring your attention to your breathing. More importantly, find something that could feel delicate and soft in your breath. It could take a few minutes for your breath to soften and sweeten. As you start to relax your breath, it quietens a little.

From here you will very quickly start to be flooded with the usual thoughts, sensations or emotions. Firstly, reassure yourself that this is good - this is part of the process. Just sit with them.

What starts to happen is that one sensation will become the clearest. It may be a thought or a sensation or an emotion.

*From here you are going to **do** something – you are going to **fully allow** this feeling. If it helps, say "I fully allow this feeling".*

As you really allow it, watch it take its course. It may become

20

stronger – allow that. It may soften – allow that. More likely it will become replaced by another emotion or a deeper feeling.

This will probably go on for eight to ten different emotions or feelings or thoughts. Just keep allowing and try to just start to observe them - observe their coming and going. Maybe see them as clouds across the perfect blue sky of your mind. What may happen is that everything may just go quiet, even for a few seconds and then the thoughts will start again.

Just remember that quiet moment, that sense of the clear blue sky in the mind.

These feelings and thoughts or body sensations can at certain times feel intense. The important thing to realize is that these feelings are just trying to move, to shift from being locked in you. Just continue to allow them, just let them be and try to glimpse the quietness, the blue sky, behind them. That quietness is you and the thoughts, feelings and sensations are just overlaying patterns.

In time and with practice, these quiet moments will start to increase. It's important not to let your mind think of this! Just accept what is happening right now and don't think about goals and achievements.

All you are doing is allowing and observing - that is it. This process sounds easy, but it can be challenging at first. Take your time here, just do a few moments here and there and come back to it.

This process will eventually allow you to move through being overwhelmed by feelings, emotions and sensations. However, if you are really stressed, or you have a history of emotional trauma, it is much harder to achieve this to begin with. It can feel too much. In this case, it is important to get support. When we are faced with trauma and the anxiety that springs from it, we need a team of support. This includes our GP, a psychotherapist or counsellor, and a friend or trusted family member. If feeling overwhelmed at any stage - first seek support, then once this is in place carry on slowly and gently.

*[It may also feel overwhelming] if you suffer from chronic physical pain. When you start to sit quietly and practice allowing, accepting and observing, the pain can at first feel too strong. If this happens to you, do this process little by little, just practice for a few minutes a day. I have often seen these techniques work with patients of mine who are in severe chronic pain. The point is to be **slow** and **gentle** and not force things.*

Chapter 3

Timing and Tempo

Timing

There is something about perfect timing isn't there?

When you just get the feeling that you are in the right place at the right time and everything just falls into place. How rare are those moments?

Timing is key in many things, most obviously in sport. When a tennis shot is timed perfectly, it can be unstoppable! [Similarly], when we time perfectly what we are going to say in a conversation, it can have the intended impact. If we say what we want to at the key moment, it almost reaches a deeper connection with the person. If we say it too early or too late, it just won't do it.

Great actors and comedians seem to have this perfect timing, knowing just when to give that extra half second pause which engages us. But it seems very hit and miss as to whether we get the perfect timing. It feels either high skill or great luck or a combination of both.

As our skills improve, say in a sport, it becomes less like luck to hit the perfect shot. That's why practice makes our timing better and better. The same is true of public speaking. The more we do it, the better we get and the more well-timed our responses are.

What is practice though? Really, practice is just paying attention to what we are doing and repeating the activity again and again.

But what about other elements in life that seem more like luck? How can we achieve better timing and so maximize our potential in life?

We repeat actions a lot but often without perfect timing, we make mistakes again and again and often still do not learn. How can we make our timing more in sync with the movement of the universe? If we could do this everything could flow a little better.

In sports and other activities, we have identified two elements that, over time, bring better timing. Paying attention to what we are doing *and* repeating the action - both elements together constitute *practice.*

So how can we *practice at life?* We spend enough time repeating activities but one thing that often we forget to do is to *pay attention* to what we are doing.

Tempo

There is another element that could lead us to better general timing in life and this is the idea of reading and *being in tempo with life.* What does this mean? To read and be in the tempo of life we need to do a few things.

Firstly, as I've said, we need to pay attention to what we are doing. But more than that we need to start to become more aware of our environments, of the people, what they are saying when they are talking, and to what is happening in and around us, including in nature. For this, we need to start to learn to sense the world around us.

We all have wonderful senses, eyesight, hearing, touch, smell, and a sense of where our bodies are in space and time. All too often, we take these senses for granted.

The best way to engage our senses is to become fully aware of them in our environment. Just spend a few seconds with your senses.

Explore **vision** first - bring your awareness to what is in your line of vision, what is in the distance. Really become aware of what you are seeing in the moment. It's amazing how much we filter through our eyes, how much we can see. Our brains only process a tiny proportion of what we see, that which it considers important in the moment. It applies a series of filters to our vision. If our brains didn't do this, we would be in a state of being constantly overwhelmed.

The question is, though, how do we decide what is important and what is not? We learn this over our lifetime. As our vision starts to wake up as a baby, we learn to focus our attention on important objects: Mum, food, drink and things we need to be concerned about in our environment. We learn very quickly to filter out what is deemed unimportant.

As we grow, our visual priorities change with our developing consciousness. We learn to pay attention to other factors like our living environments and finding potential mates. Our senses are driven by quite basic human requirements.

If you think about an indigenous hunter or trapper, they learn over years to see what we don't, for example, the tiny changes in the environment, which indicate a recent animal passage.

They learn to pay attention to those almost invisible varying elements.

From here, just spend a moment with your **hearing**. Allow your hearing to take in all the sounds, near and far. Isn't it amazing how much we screen out of what we see and hear, feel and smell? As before, with our vision, we must screen a lot of what our senses are telling us moment to moment in order not to feel overwhelmed by these senses.

It is clever how our brains just put most of what we sense into the background. We are only alerted when something new is noticed, which sends a fresh signal to the brain and wakes up our attention to the moment.

But if our attention is somewhere else - my attention right now is on what I'm writing, but if I stop, I can hear beautiful early morning spring birdsong, an incredibly beautiful sound. So right now, I'm trying to write and listen. This slows me down and enlivens the writing process.

But, for me, to be in tempo with life I have to slow down to this natural pace. This is a place where my senses are *moved* by the moment, that change in light as the sun rises, that change in birdsong right now.

An amazing thing happens when I start to be *In Tempo* with life through nature. It feels like my brain softens, my need to finish this chapter falls away and I relax and start to enjoy the moment.

When this happens I really slow down and relax and don't really want to type – I could easily just sit here, hearing, feeling and seeing nature, and now becoming aware of the deep stillness behind it. In this place all is well, I always feel safe, held by life and I have no drive to do anything. It's a beautiful place and one could really see from here how the teacher Eckhart Tolle could sit on a park bench in London for two years, quite content!

It seems that to get into tempo with things, an important access point is to become aware of our senses, and to pay attention to our environment. This immediately takes us out of the world of abstract thinking to something more real.

This process can slow us down, but it can also do the opposite. Nature isn't necessarily slow - everything isn't a sloth. It can be very rapid, whilst also being unlaboured by thinking. Animals don't think about something – they act in the moment, senses totally awake and aware. If we tune into our senses and open our awareness, we have more chance of acting *in tempo* with life.

Let's start to explore these ideas. We will come back to our senses in a much deeper way later.

CONTEMPLATION 3

Timing and Tempo

For this contemplation, we don't need to sit. We can do this whilst walking to work or even sitting on the loo!

Let's start by bringing your attention to your vision. What can you see directly in front of you, right now? Don't move your head or eyes. Just see what is beyond the book or screen you are looking at.

Now take in your surroundings for a second, see the colours, shapes and objects around you, and see your horizon. Enjoy all the different colours and shapes of things. Do not think about anything you see, just look and do not judge, just enjoy the looking. It's quite nice, isn't it?

Next, let your awareness come to your hearing. What is your landscape of sound around you now? What is in the background? It's amazing how many background sounds we filter out. I often find that even in a busy city, the sounds of nature are still there behind the noise. But don't filter out the noises you don't like, just allow your awareness to take them in and not judge them. See if you can hear a quieter humming behind the noises, almost a stillness behind the sounds. Really enjoy these sounds and let them in unfiltered by thinking about them.

Now just spend a second feeling the floor under your feet, or the chair under your bottom. Can you feel the sense of the book you are holding or device you are looking at: how do they feel?

As we spend a few minutes on these simple ways to explore our vision, hearing and touch, what may start to happen is that our thinking brain can start to get quiet. Maybe, just for a moment, we are in the present, we are not in the land of concepts, thinking future or past but right here, breathing softly and aware of our environment.

*Now I want you to open your awareness to **all these senses at once**. Let's call this sensory awareness **Nature Sense**. It's tricky at first, you may only do it for a second or so but keep trying.*

*Now once you can spend a few seconds trying to feel **Nature Sense**, what I want you to sense is if there is a tempo to it? A natural rhythm. Just ask the question and be open to the answer. What I mean by tempo is that if we really open our senses to the environment can we start to feel some sense of coherence between all these sounds, sights and senses? Is there a quality that can link them, maybe some underlying quietness under all these sensations connecting ourselves and all of them? I don't want you to think about this, just try to feel it - let's call that our **Felt-Sense**.*

If you are finding this difficult, don't worry, we are at the beginning. We are looking at starting to change the way our senses interact with our brains. This sensing is beyond conceptual thinking – it's like feeling life through nature. It can be difficult at the beginning, but we can all do this eventually.

Finding this rhythm may start us on the path into greater timing and tempo. But we need to practice and to slowly awaken our senses.

In the history of the world, many ancient indigenous tribes have been documented as being able to use their senses in extraordinary ways. So maybe this Nature Sense is something in which we can start to deepen our own sensory awareness. Maybe these ancient practices are within our ancestral indigenous collective memory and with which we can reconnect.

In this practice, we will start to learn to develop our senses and our sensory awareness. This will hopefully connect us more deeply with nature, ourselves and others. We will be developing these ideas and hopefully our felt-sense as we go on.

Chapter 4

The Gift of the Present

When we see young children playing, it is such a beautiful sight. They seem to have no agenda, are unfettered by what society says, or by how they *should* act and be in the world. Their attention is solely on what they are doing. It doesn't matter if they are playing in a beautiful garden or in the street. They are inquisitive, free and totally in the moment. How often do we as adults take time to play, just to be in the moment, to laugh freely and to have some good old fun?

As we start to understand what our neutral point is, a natural consequence is that we are brought more into the present. Our mind still wanders to the future and the past, but more time is spent in the here and now. In this state, time can feel like it is slowing down. As a consequence, we can start to get a sense that we have more time for things. How does that work?!

It seems we spend much of our waking time in potential future or past universes, thinking and planning potential futures, different potential scenarios or analyzing what has happened: was it good or good enough, did we upset someone, or we are sometimes feeling regret, or anger about the past, or fear for the future. If we really look at this, it seems such a waste of time!

Of course, we must plan our day, of course we must review the past – otherwise how would we learn from it? Of course, we should remember beautiful memories of love and those sweet moments in life, but living in these places doesn't allow for the beauty of the moment. I like the phrases *take time to smell the roses* and *wake up and smell the coffee*! They bring to mind the idea of being in the present moment.

The danger for us is that if we spend all our time in future planning or past analysis, we don't spend enough time in the present moment, spontaneous and free to be - to be playful, to observe, to let our senses breathe and to sense life.

There is a beautiful garden at one of my practices that takes my breath away with its beauty. However oftentimes, people pass through it and don't even see it – with our minds either in the future or past, we actually miss out on incredible and beautiful things that are happening right now.

Isn't technology wonderful? A huge proportion of us own a *smart phone*. Having a smart phone means that we have access to a huge amount of information, worldwide, just by the touch of a button. I am amazed at how quickly we can research almost anything. The danger is, though, that we can get lost in this world of information and sensory stimulation.

I love technology and the world it has opened for me, but I must police it with myself and my three teenagers: we have had dinners where all four of us are playing with our mobile phones. They are banned at dinner now, unless there is something specific that we want to research to aid our conversation!

How wonderful it is to just sit and be, just to stop, to have no agenda, just for a few moments, to *smell* the roses, *look* at the sky, *feel* the softness of our breath, *hear* the wind, *watch* the leaves - even watch a plane cruising above us!

Usually the only time we are brought into the present moment is when we are in sharp distress. As we have discussed, in an emergency, our nervous systems are super-awake, our senses are more acute and alive, and our adrenalin is pumping. In these situations, our bodies respond by pumping out a variety of hormones including adrenaline, and cortisol. Our nervous systems wake up and are on full alert. We smell, hear and see more acutely and our hearts beat faster, ready for action.

In this way, we - and most animals - have adapted to perceived threats. It works because our super-awareness alerts us to dangers. For animals, it is awareness to predators. For us, it is awareness to dangerous situations. In these moments, our senses are alive and alert.

We are brought directly into the present, so we can respond to the danger. This is a vital instinct deep within our body functions, governed by the more primitive parts of the brain in the brain stem. Of course, the problem in modern life of overstimulation to the senses means that our systems are on full alert. The strange thing with this is that we are not brought into the moment - quite the opposite, we are deeply distracted. This is confusing for our minds and body.

Here, in the Dynamics of Stillness training, we are going to start to untangle this body/mind mix up, which will serve to calm down this response. It will start to allow us to live more in the present and eventually to centre ourselves in Stillness.

Even in key moments in life, sometimes it can be hard to really remain present and take in the full beauty of those precious times.

How wonderful would it be - and deeply calming - to be able to just live in the moment, even for a few minutes each day? How wonderful would it to be able just to be in the moment, even to feel breathed and moved by life in the moment with all its wonder, pain and beauty?

CONTEMPLATION 4

Sitting in the Present

Let's build a little on what we have been practicing. In a way we are in training to retrain our brain and senses towards coming from a place of deep stillness.

Let's try now to take a few minutes each day to sit and really be in the present. It helps if you can concentrate on the softness of your breathing for a few minutes, building on what we have already practiced. Just look at something that feels soft in your breath. You can do this even if you have difficulty in breathing or if you suffer from anxiety. Breathe softly, not deeply, and allow your outbreath to be slightly longer than your inbreath. You have plenty of air.

Next, we really let those thoughts come and go. It can be helpful to see these thoughts as clouds across a beautiful blue sky, the sky being your mind and the thoughts being clouds, whether they are grey thunder clouds or even beautiful wispy white clouds, whether they come, or they go. Behind these clouds, the sky is still there and always will be. What is this blue sky? This blue sky behind the thoughts, feelings and sensations is you! And this has a Stillness to it.

Once you begin to feel the internal thoughts and noises start to quieten, allow your mind to take in your surroundings. Start with the sounds, whether they are loud and irritating - even if there is loud banging of a power tool outside, or heavy traffic, or if it's the songbirds in full voice, it doesn't matter - just allow them and listen. Listen without judging any of them, just allow them to arise and to fall away.

After a few minutes let your eyes take in your surroundings, let your view move unhindered - do not control it, let it move wherever it wants to. Maybe now, let your eyes go to the minute detail of the crumb on the floor or to the vista and horizon. Just let your vision be moved by the moment.

Next, just start to bring awareness to your sense of smell. We usually don't use this sense except when new aromas come into our consciousness. Everyday smells fade into the background just as everyday sounds do. When you bring awareness to your sense of smell, everyday smells are treated by the brain as new, different and important.

Finally, spend a few minutes feeling things in your environment. Pick up an object and enjoy feeling its texture and contours. If you are near water, whether it is a stream or just a sink (if it is the sink, fill it with water) and spend a few minutes just feeling the water, moving your hands through it and enjoying the texture, temperature and fluidity.

Now take a few minutes to enjoy all your senses. Just let your senses direct what they want to do, whether you are drawn to a sight, smell, sound or a texture. Just let yourself be moved by the moment. Allow your mind to really be in this present moment. Whatever it brings up just observe, allow and accept.

Now close your eyes if you wish and just allow yourself to sit in the quiet of the moment and just be for a few moments.

If we can just spend five minutes a day retraining your brain to be in the moment, it can bring many rewards.

As we go back to normal life, we find that spontaneously we can have brought back to the present moment by our senses – this is a wonderful feeling!

Those roses can really start to smell great, those children playing can distract us, and maybe the mental chatter of thought, feeling and sensation can quieten just a little bit and allow your brain to quietly breathe.

Enjoy.

Chapter 5

Developing a Practice

In the two great traditions of spiritual practice that are Buddhism and Taoism (or Daoism), teachers over generations have talked about the idea of letting go of attachments and desires. Attachments are what links us to the past, be it attachment to relationships, power or money. Desires are all about the future, our future wishes and dreams. Attachment and desire both keep us either in the future or the past.

I have heard many times teachers within these traditions telling their students to let go of attachment and desire.

In my experience this is much easier said than done! It is a relatively easy concept to think about, but the reality of letting go of both is much harder - especially today! In my experience, if we try to achieve this, if we try at all we slip in to the *desire* mode, meaning this wish to do something overcomes our ability to actually do it! So on goes the cycle.

Over the years, I have found that the only way for me to start to achieve this is by developing a practice. I find that by applying concepts and thoughts about these subjects I achieve the opposite of what I am looking for. I prefer doing something

Practice and, with regularity, this can start me on the path to letting go of attachment and desire.

In the last session we started to bring our minds into a neutral place and then we explored what our senses are taking in right now. Through this, we are brought into the present moment, not by conceptualizing but by feeling it.

I feel it is vital for us all to develop some sort of daily practice, even if for just five or ten minutes at first and slowly building up our skill base.

It is very like a musician. We cannot learn an instrument if we don't practice - believe me I've tried! If we practice five minutes a day, slowly we will progress, but a highly skilled classical musician may need to practice for four to five hours per day to perfect their art. Now I'm not asking you to practice for four to five hours a day, but just to apply these techniques, meditations, and sensory experiences for just a few minutes a day. I am hoping, over time, you will start to feel the positive effects of your developing practice and naturally want to spend a little more time enjoying these new experiences of sense and feeling.

Preserving this allotted time to develop your practice is really time for you to come back to yourself, come into your body and reconnect with the moment, your Health and the great tides that move through us - more about that in the next few chapters!

Practice 5

Finding a Time to Practice

With this time, I want you to sit quietly, comfortably and tune in to the softness in your breathing, allowing, accepting and observing everything that comes up and just bring your attention gently back to your breath.

If you are struggling with any part of this just accept that you are finding it difficult, then just soften your shoulders, your chest, your hips, relaxing your physical body as much as you can and then refocus on your breath.

Once you start to feel your brain softening and becoming neutral and relaxing, I want you to ask your body what time would be best to spend ten to fifteen minutes a day on developing your practice. For each of us a different time will suit.

I like to do these techniques twice a day. First thing in the morning before I get up, and secondly, in the early evening after I finish work and before dinner. I find that practicing at these times sets me up at the beginning of the day and relaxes me at the end of the day.

It is best to play about with it - often it is a matter of finding a *few quiet minutes, especially if you have young children, when you are either constantly on the go or too exhausted to do anything. If you have young kids, then it's almost **more** important to find those ten minutes: it will allow you to deal with your day easier and **everyone** will benefit!*

If you can, make a pact with yourself to spend ten minutes a day developing your practice.

Good luck!

Chapter 6

Posture

Let's talk for a moment about postures. I have said that you can do this work in any posture as it is mainly perceptual work. I wish to talk a bit about posture when we are sitting down.

Buddhist, Daoist and Hindu traditions tend to employ similar sitting practice positions called, in various traditions, *full lotus* position or *pyramid* posture. In this posture, as depicted in statues of the Buddha of Compassion, the heels are turned upwards towards the face. This is not easy to do unless you are very flexible, or you have been in training.

A lot of meditational practices talk of sitting through the pain and hours of discomfort sitting in this posture or as close as you can get. I have done this many times, with varying degrees of success.

My legs are much more supple now than when I was a child and teenager, but I still lose feeling in them after being in a classic sitting posture for too long. The positives of sitting with legs crossed, to some degree, is that we have a wide base: the idea of a pyramid, with our legs and open hips forming the base and the top of our head is the apex. This gives a good spinal posture.

As an osteopath, I am very aware of the importance of freedom in the spinal joints positively affecting the nerve supply to the internal organs. Each spinal segment has a variety of nerve roots and paths that pass through each segment. Freedom within each segment seems to help with freedom in these nerves and through the nerves to the actual blood supply itself and to the internal organs. It makes sense that many of the traditions advocate good spinal posture.

The problem with sitting in chairs is that we tend to slump in them, dropping our spines and compressing parts of them. If we sit with our hips apart, it naturally makes the spine want to straighten. This is a good start. From here, we can start to lengthen the spine.

The Daoists would talk of the pyramid posture being vital for energy to start to flow naturally in the energy channels which they believed were central in the body - the large central meridians. As one would sink into the pyramidal form, it would allow energy to naturally rise and be transformed. Also, if sitting correctly, we tend to be able to breathe more easily and the quality of our breathing is better. If our spines are straight, the big muscle of breathing - the diaphragm - can sit freely and move more naturally, allowing the mechanism of breathing to be stronger and freer. This becomes important as our practice develops.

If we allow our *sitting bones* to really contact the surface on which we sit, it helps to give us a sense of grounding, of being connected more strongly to the earth. This is also important.

So, in summary, yes, we can practice in any position: my first daily practice is with me lying supine (on my back) in bed. However, if we practice lying down when we are tired, we can fall asleep very quickly - which is OK, but we still need to do our practice!

We can do these techniques standing up on the underground, we can do them whilst running - which I do often. I practice them whilst painting, and while I am treating patients - in fact, in any situation. I also think it serves to spend ten minutes a day developing a sitting practice.

Practice 6

Sitting Position

First, find a comfortable room that is quiet and, hopefully, where you won't be disturbed. Switch off your phone - just for ten minutes! Bring a glass of water in case of you become thirsty.

Often the best place to practice is on the softness of a sofa, a bed, or a comfy chair, but the floor is also perfectly fine. For comfort, I tend to put a pillow under my bottom – this means my legs don't pull when I cross them. You can use as many pillows or rolled up towels as you need to feel comfortable.

You may also need to place a rolled-up towel under each knee to support them and reduce the pulling effect that occurs when you are sitting like this. Above all, make yourself as comfortable as you can.

Notes:

1. The more you practice, the less supports you will need.

2. If you have hip restrictions or knee or back problems just sit straight on a good chair with feet on the floor.

3. You don't need to sit in full or half lotus unless you are able to do so easily.

Now you are sitting down comfortably, let's begin to straighten the spine and bring a degree of balance to our body. Firstly, soften your breathing and relax your body. Is there anywhere in your body that feels tight or uncomfortable? If so, move a little and try to direct your outbreath towards the area. As you breathe out, relax that part and try to feel as if you are breathing out the tightness.

As you begin to feel more comfortable and relaxed, try firstly to feel the area where your head meets your neck at the back. This, in most of us, is locked - the head tends to sit back on the neck and lock it down. See this space between the head and neck and gently nod your head down. As you look more downwards towards the floor, it opens the space between your head and neck. When we start to sit, we tend to need to open this space and we start to look downwards more. Ideally, we want to look at a point a couple of metres in front of us and sustain it.

Just enjoy the sense of space between your head and neck – it's quite relaxing! Once we open this space, we tend to find the rest of our neck lengthens a bit to compensate. Allow your neck to lengthen. It may help to visualize a string attached to the crown of your head exerting a gentle pull upwards, very gently and slowly.

Now, hopefully, you will start to sense the spine

lengthening from the top down. Enjoy the sense of space coming and, for any stuck bits, just breathe out the tension and always try to soften and lengthen at the same time.

Next, feel the spine lengthening between your shoulders. As it lengthens, allow your shoulders to widen as if they could hang freely. Allow your chest just to relax and sink just a little, soften it and breathe out any tensions.

Now let your stomach soften and your breathing to relax. Start to feel your lower back lengthening from the top down and your pelvis start to relax. As you do this, you should find that your hips naturally want to widen. As your hips widen, let your legs soften and relax, all the way down to your feet and toes.

What we are doing here is relaxing but lengthening and straightening our spine so that our organs can enjoy a free nerve and blood supply. This, too, will help us as we deepen our practice.

Just enjoy sitting here in comfort, observing the softness in your breath, accepting, allowing and observing anything that comes up in your mind in terms of thoughts, feelings and sensations. There is a sense here of understanding that each thought or feeling or sensation is connected to either an attachment from the past or a desire for the future. Never judge these sensation, just watch them pass across your blue sky or your blank canvas.

Try to enjoy just sitting there. After a while, a sensation of discomfort will arise - it always does. Just observe this for a few moments, then stop there, don't fight through it. Your time tolerance will improve by the day.

47

Chapter 7

The Stillness Behind Everything

We live in a world full of noise, where it is hard to find real silence. Even in wild places there are the birds singing and the noise of the wind. Occasionally, if you wake up in the hour before dawn, in the quiet of the night, you can experience a real stillness. This stillness has a particular quality - aliveness, a power. You can sense it, not just with your ears, but with your whole body. The quality of it is amazing, it is still, but there is a huge dynamic energy to it. What is this power in it?

Similarly, sometimes mountaineers describe a sense of this real stillness way up high in the snow, when the winds drop and sometimes they become enveloped by a huge silent stillness. They describe this silence as powerful, almost overwhelming. They say it almost feels like sensing the throb of the universe, and when we feel this stillness, it can feel possible to feel connected to the whole universe.

In Hindu and Buddhist religions they talk of the *ohm* sound, the sound of the universe humming or the underlying love that connects all. They sometimes chant this sound as part of their meditation.

Is it possible to sense this quality in our everyday lives? Can you imagine how we could feel if our senses were connected to this quality at all times? To sense this stillness, we must first quieten our internal noise, the sound of the relentless actions and reactions of our minds.

As we start to find a Quiet Neutral in ourselves, an amazing thing starts to happen. Our senses that have been bombarded and in a constant sense of being overwhelmed can start to become quiet, soften and open, as if they can really start to breathe. As this happens, we start to really hear that bird singing and sometimes to almost sense *why* it is singing. As this neutral develops in ourselves, and as we practice, it becomes easier to start to sense a great Stillness that is always there, behind the sounds, in the background. We can start to feel it in our body and to hear it.

It's an odd concept really. How can we hear stillness? Surely that means an absence of sound? I think tuning in to stillness engages a different part of our sense of hearing - almost on a different vibration. It is a kind of *felt-sense* that we feel and hear together. It is difficult to explain but easier to sense.

We all use our senses slightly differently, when we try sensing things that live on the edge of our perception, like sensing stillness.

For me it helps to try to hear a certain quality of sound. I can, at first, access this with my hearing. From here, it can be possible to go on to sense it with my whole body.

To try to get a sense of stillness, I firstly let myself be present to all the sounds around me, then I try to hear or feel something quiet *behind* those sounds. The sound, for me, is not quite a hiss but between a hiss and a throb - maybe a quiet hum - but the feeling you get when you hear it is one of **power**. So, maybe, a quiet, powerful hum. When you start to hear and feel this, you will have your own way of describing it. Also, it varies as to its quality, albeit slightly. I wonder if that is because the sound or feeling changes, or more likely that our senses vary a little in their function.

This great stillness that is always there has a quality of peace to it. In Tibetan Buddhism, there is a practice called *resting in the great natural peace*, which is similar.

As we develop our practice here, I am interested in engaging and developing our ability to shift our perception so that eventually it is free to be moved by the moment and the great tides and stillness around us. Here we are not looking for internal stillness but learning to perceive a stillness that is always there around and outside us, but also in us.

So, in this technique, we start with our awareness around us and see if we can experience a similar sense within ourselves. This is a way we can calm ourselves when we are irritable or upset, or it can be a way of starting a meditation.

The best thing about this work is that it just feels great, so as we connect more to stillness and can learn to directly access it at any moment, our body/mind wants more connection. So, naturally, a five-minute sitting or standing meditation will expand to thirty or forty minutes without us having to force it - it just feels nice!

Contemplation 7

The Stillness Behind Everything

Sit quietly, ideally in not too noisy a place at the beginning. It is easiest in nature but once we get good at this it is possible to sense this quiet wherever you are. Even in loud and distressing situations, if we can learn to tune in to this sense of underlying stillness, it can become deeply calming to ourselves and even to others near us.

As you sit, spend a few minutes turning your awareness to the quietness, softness and delicacy in your breathing. Let all thoughts come and then let them go, passing like clouds, all the while letting your attention naturally return to the softness in your breathing. If you slightly lengthen your outbreath so it is longer than the inbreath, this calms your system quicker.

With each outbreath, allow yourself to relax your body more, breathing out any tension in either your mind or body. Focus on breathing in sweet softness and breathing out tensions. As your sense of neutral comes, your body starts to relax. It is almost as if the tight grip your mind has on your body starts to relax and soften, and your senses start to open. Let your thoughts and sensations come and go, not focusing too deeply on them. Just watch them come and go. Try not to focus even on the developing sense of quiet in you. Fully **allow** everything and let your mind breathe.

From this point, bring your attention to your hearing. Let yourself be aware of all the sounds, from the plumbing, to the birds, to your tummy rumbling. Let these sounds arise and then sense the quiet between the sounds. It is almost as if the sounds arise and fall away within the quiet.

Sense, not just with your ears and hearing, but with your whole body. Sense the quiet behind the sounds. Maybe you will start to get a sense of that great stillness that lies behind everything. It has a tonal quality that you feel as much as hear. It is beautiful and deeply calming, yet so very alive.

At the beginning we can only get a few seconds of sensing this. If we sit with it and our bodies learn to recognize and respond to it, this great stillness can stay with us for longer and longer periods. Our mind and bodies really love sensing this stillness. It can sometimes start to give us the sensation that we are being held by life and that all is well. A sense of resting in the great natural peace.

Chapter 8

Pure Attention

How often do we give something our full attention? Hardly ever really these days. If we are eating, we are also talking and checking our texts, if we are watching TV, we are talking and eating, if we are walking the dog we are on the telephone or thinking about something we must do tomorrow. When are we really present to the activity we are undertaking? It's rare that we are - and getting rarer!

As a child, I remember watching a craftsperson at work or somebody doing something they were skilled at and loved. As they focused their attention completely, and abandoned themselves to the task at hand, it seemed that they generated a gentle, sweet energy – it was literally palpable. I wanted to be around them as they worked, and I didn't want to leave. I remember sensing that energy as a young child and I am still drawn to it today.

That sweet, soft energy seems to be generated by total attention and pure awareness, without a splitting or scattering of intent - pure energy- focused on the task at hand. It is wonderful to experience! The energy feels a bit like love - and what could feel better?

The opposite, of course, can be true. If we are emotional, be it happy or sad, if our nervous systems are on full alert and we are distressed about something, then the energy around us is disturbed. It is easy to sense this energy. If, for example, you are in a queue next to a person who is distressed, it feels uncomfortable. You almost want to remove yourself from the place. When we are in these alert states, it does not matter how beautiful the sunset is in front of us, we don't fully see it. We may glance up and register it, but we do not really feel and take in its beauty - it seems impossible at that moment for us to be moved by it.

What is it to be moved by something? Why do people say that something *moves* them? Maybe, to be moved by something, it is like there is a connection to a deep part of us that is moved or engaged by that sunset, or a story, or there is a moment of grace.

What if we could train our brains to have less noise in amongst stress and distress, so that we can be still enough to *smell the roses* more of the time? How much more beautiful could life be?

How often do we approach anything in life with pure attention? How often do we meet an object or a person without any preconceived ideas about them? How often do we really look at a tree or object without naming, quantifying, or judging it? How much of our lives is spent reacting to our ideas and thoughts about a person or a loved one without really seeing them in the moment? When we do this, we are relating to concepts and not real things. This is harmful to us, as it disconnects us from one another and from nature.

It is so hard not to react to patterns of behaviour in friends and family, but the more we are aware of our reactions, the less we enter conflict with them.

Becoming aware of our reactions is the basis of psychotherapy and cognitive behavioural therapies, but it only goes halfway. We need to step beyond this and let go of all concepts of another person so that we can meet them totally free of any history of reaction and any concepts. This seems almost an impossible task! But if we can go a little bit in that direction, it would open a great deal of beauty to us – in relationship to one another and, again, to nature.

When we give whatever we are doing our full attention, something amazing happens. The activity brings a sense of stillness within its motion and generates a beautiful energy. This is something which other people want to be around. It brings us into a state of pure awareness, without our energy being in too many places at once.

If our thoughts and emotions are in many directions, each thought and emotion and feeling has energy, so our energy is lost in many different directions. This dispersal of energy is exhausting! If our energy is clear, it will make whatever activity we are doing more enjoyable and we become better at it!

Wild animals, of course, give what they are doing their full and undivided attention. A cheetah in full flight hunting is the epitome of stillness in action, running at sixty miles an hour with its full awareness and attention on its prey, but there is a quiet stillness within its extreme activity. The same of course is true of top sports people. When a player is on top form, there can sometimes seem a palpable stillness about their action. It is wonderful to watch!

When teaching osteopaths to really understand the nature of anatomy, I try to help them to open out their senses and to feel subtle processes within the body. I start by trying to de-educate them. We learn anatomy by looking at books and seeing dissections. When doing so, we are learning from something that is either two-dimensional and it is certainly not living, breathing tissue - which looks and feels totally different. The danger for the student is that she or he can apply concepts to what she is trying to feel and, in doing so, could limit her perception and her ability to feel processes in living tissue.

So, when studying, we try to let go of concepts and pictures and try to really **feel**. It's hard to do at the beginning, but if I encourage them to be creative and think of colour, shape and emotion, they often start to get a sense of the living tissue below their hands. Over time, the students start to feel the living anatomy and perceptual clarity can start to develop.

Let's now try to let go of any concepts, if we can – this is hard to do but if we can do it just a little bit, it can open us up to a new level of awareness and perception.

Let's also work with being present enough to give whatever we are doing our full attention, to really be present to what we are doing or who or what we are relating to.

Contemplation 8

Pure Attention

For this contemplation, we can be anywhere - inside or outside. Try it in a few different locations and see what works well for you. It is easier, in the beginning, to try it in nature - for example, looking at a tree or a flower, ideally something not moving too much at first - or you can do it by looking at any object indoors.

Don't put pressure on yourself to perform this contemplation perfectly. What we really are looking for is a softening of our conceptual grip on judging what we see, which could give some space for a purer awareness.

First, identify an object that you are going engage with. Once you have done this, sit quietly as before. Let your nervous system settle, allow all thoughts, but slowly bring your awareness to your breath, something soft in the feeling of the breath, or something soft and fluid in the body.

When you start to settle, just allow your senses to feel the underlying stillness behind everything. This sense is almost audible - it feels like it is on the edge of our hearing. Once you get a sense of this, it becomes easier each time to tune into.

From here, allow your awareness to rest on the chosen object. Try to let go of any judgments or concepts of the object. Let go of any knowledge you have acquired about it and even any words which could have formed a screen between you and the object you are looking at.

Try to really see it as if you are seeing it for the first time. Try to see the object with all your energy, your whole being and awareness. If you can do this, you may start to become aware of a sense of clear awareness. This brings a certain stillness and energy to it, just pure clear attention.

It is hard to keep this awareness up. At the beginning, just for a few seconds, our minds really want to wander and attach themselves to many things. If this happens, just allow it and don't judge it. This is normal. Bring your awareness back to the flower or whatever you are looking at.

This awareness can bring a sense of awe and even a sense of love. Try to just spend a couple of minutes at this exercise each day, then try to bring the concept into other areas.

A great practice is to **really** listen, with an open mind and an open heart to whomever you are talking to, just listen without preparing your thoughts for the next thing you will say.

How rarely do we really listen - I mean really hear what another is saying - letting go of concepts, analysis or anything? How often do we just sit in quiet stillness and listen?

Amazingly, this open-hearted listening becomes a blessing - not just for you but for the person talking to you! It is a wonderful thing to be heard, really heard!

You can do this with your other senses. You can really smell - what does that perfume smell like? It's funny, but we have no descriptions for smells in themselves, meaning we must compare smells to other smells - for example, it smells **like a flower**.

If we really feel whatever we are touching, the experience can be like an act of love. To touch lovingly - even if it is our mobile phone! The interesting thing is that when we apply pure attention, our touch softens a little and it naturally slows down.

If we widen our focus and try this in other areas, for example, cooking supper with pure attention, only focusing on the task at hand. What happens? Does the food taste better?

It's nice to bathe with pure attention: to feel the water from the shower or tap cleansing your body is very enjoyable, or to become aware of the sensations of the water on your skin.

Driving with pure attention tends to mean we slow down a bit and enjoy the experience in our mind more. If we try driving with no destination in mind, the pure attention naturally brings presence with it, being present to the moment and this brings a natural sense of quiet, peaceful stillness.

Another example is walking or running with pure awareness. Our steps get lighter and softer and we connect more to the earth below us. A lovely trick is to walk **love** into the earth, meaning each step taken implants a feeling of love onto the earth. The earth loves this, and so will you! It is amazing to run with pure attention. The running, although we are in movement, has a quality of stillness like a cheetah running.

We can practice pure attention doing absolutely anything. Life can become a practice, meaning you can start to be in a constant process of internal cultivation. The more we do it, the more benefits are felt. It's just a case of remembering to do it a few times a day until you develop the habit of it and it becomes integrated into your reality.

Chapter 9

Natural Stillpoints

Sometimes, when we are in the middle of a good chat with someone and both parties have said what they want to say, there is a sense of an agreement in an idea or a way forward. What can happen at this point is that both parties can go quiet, just for a short time, and there is a special moment between you of quiet stillness. This is a Stillpoint.

This Stillpoint can be experienced if we are working hard at a task and suddenly it seems like the world around us goes quiet, our mind becomes still, and a sense of peace comes over us. It seems like a pause in events when everything settles quite naturally. We don't induce these magic moments; they seem to come naturally to us.

The interesting quality about these moments is that the Stillpoint can happen within each of us, or between us if we are with another person. It can even happen in a whole room full of people, for example, in a lecture situation or after hearing a wonderful piece of music at a concert. The Stillpoint seems to happen both *within* and *around* us. It is as if the worlds goes quiet for a moment of rest and re-balance before going on its way.

The Stillpoint has a different quality than that of sensing the Natural Stillness that is always there, as we did in a previous exercise. Here we are not actively sensing the Stillness. In these moments, it is almost as if the Stillness meets **us**. It seems to break into our consciousness - it comes from the background to the foreground.

Maybe these Stillpoints are when our thoughts and actions become quiet enough so that the underlying stillness can move from the background to the forefront of our awareness. It is almost more than that, it is like at the Stillpoint, the world around us and ourselves come to a point of stillness and something seems to reorganize itself - a process of transmutation occurs. A Stillpoint has an inherent energy within it, and afterwards things are just a little bit different, the world has changed just a little bit, or something in our awareness has shifted slightly.

These moments seem to be precipitated by an action or a thought which quietens as the Stillpoint enters. It can almost feel like the universe is forming a resolution in these moments, like a deep rebalancing. This is quite wonderful to witness and I'm sure all of us have witnessed it occasionally.

It would be wonderful for those moments to happen much more often, rather than as a rare moment's gift. How can we precipitate such moments more regularly? I think the answer to this question lies in firstly being aware that these moments can and do happen. If an activity or a conversation takes on a natural pause, then we can let it do so without cutting it short and filling the space with words and activity. If we just let the natural rhythm and tempo of things take its course without forcing the tempo, it can happen. If we try not to always fill the gaps, let silences be silences when they arise, it will give more chance for the Stillpoint to arise and fall away.

Great public speakers like Ex-President Obama make good use

of the natural pauses in speeches. These pauses allow the full emphasis of what has been said to sink in. If you look at Obama – for example, in his keynote speech which introduced him to the world at the 2004 Democratic National Convention - you can see that he often stopped and waited, just for a second or a fraction of a second, for words to take effect. Winston Churchill did the same in his great war speeches on the radio - the silence between his words crackling with anticipation.

If we start with allowing natural pauses to occur, even a little, they may naturally develop into Stillpoints. When they do develop into Stillpoints, it feels like they take on a natural power. If we start to get a sense of when natural pauses come within an activity, and then learn just to wait in the pauses, we may repeatedly be rewarded with the peace and connection that Stillpoints offer.

Contemplation 9

Stillpoints

For this contemplation, I want you to try to do this in two ways:

1. *Firstly, I want you to undertake a simple domestic activity which you quite like to do. For example, polishing your shoes, washing up or ironing. As you approach this physical activity, do it consciously. Pay close attention to what you are doing as we did in the last chapter. Concentrate on the task at hand. Be fully present to it with pure attention.*
   If your mind gets distracted don't let that disturb you, just gently bring your attention back to what you are doing. Try to appreciate the rhythm of the task and not get attached to the result. From here, just let yourself be open to natural pauses in the activity and, as the pauses occur, get a sense of the stillness that is there between the active moments. Let the pause develop, maybe into a Still Moment or maybe into a Stillpoint.

2. *Try to do this within a conversation. Choose a conversation with a loved one, one that hopefully isn't going to be stressful! Let the conversation take its own rhythm. Give a little bit of your attention to* **watching** *this rhythm, to watching the natural flow within the conversation. As we did in the last chapters, really listen with fully attention to the person you are communicating with, using pure attention.*

When the conversation comes to a natural pause, try not to fill the gap. Let the silence ensue. Though the other party may not be aware of it, you can be aware of what you are doing and not doing. When there is a natural pause, allow your awareness to sense the stillness between the words. You can talk too but slow down the process just that little bit and allow the conversation to breathe and soften so that it can develop natural pauses and form. Here a Stillpoint may develop, interestingly, especially if both parties reach an understanding or agreement, which seems to usher in the Stillpoint.

Try to allow these natural pauses and Stillpoints to become part of your day, whatever you are doing. It will soon develop your natural connection to an underlying stillness and bring calm and some degree of clarity. It will also sweeten your communication with others.

As we develop these processes, we are starting to recognize a natural state of neutral. Funnily enough, this means we will be more aware when we are stressed, but we will also more present to ourselves and so we can change things more quickly. By allowing, accepting and observing, we are cultivating more self-acceptance. By increasing our awareness of timing and tempo, sensing the present moment and learning to sense the Great Natural Stillness that surrounds and perfuses us, and becoming aware of Stillpoints and the natural pauses in everyday activities and interactions with other people, we start to re-pattern the way our nervous systems relate to ourselves and the world. This will start to bring you a calmness and tranquility and to your actions.

This is only the beginning. From here we will start to develop our sensory awareness to the fluidity in us, the fluid fields and natural tides in nature. We will actively deepen our connection to aspects and energies in the natural world. We will go on to start re-patterning our senses. We will learn techniques of self-healing and, eventually, for healing others.

On this journey we hope to gain a deeper connection with wholeness within ourselves, and a sense of oneness with everything.

Chapter 10

Finding Ground

We tend to live our lives in our heads, thinking and doing stuff at every waking moment.

The practices we are learning here are trying to take us away from that, to learn how to return to our senses then to take mastery of our attention and learn to fix it where we wish to, to develop our relationship to the stillness both in and around us, to become comfortable to live in the moment and to reconnect deeply to nature and its natural tides and flow.

If you think of our body literally as an energy field, where is the most energy placed when we are thinking and processing information all day? The energy must be mostly in our brain.

Actually our brains do use up most of the energy our body produces from food, there is a lot going on in there!

This can leave us ungrounded, literally as if disconnected from the earth we live on. This 'disconnection' worsens when we are not near nature and inhabit and work in buildings far from the earth.

This loss of connection energetically can make us feel 'ungrounded' almost dizzy at times.

When writing I am thinking and typing and my attention is entirely in what I am trying to say. But fortunately right now, I am in a study, which looks onto the snowy, sunny garden today.

I stop every few minutes, feel the earth beneath my feet and look at the beautiful garden. It helps me stay on subject!

I remember as a student in London, I would spend all my spare time in parks with trees. I literally became a tree hugger.

On weekends we would go to Richmond park, the closest thing to a natural, wild space that I could find, and sit by and tune into the wonderful trees there. I would find it restorative, so much so that I could 'engage with the city' again!

Trees are very grounding. In my courses I sometimes get the students to draw a tree. Mostly they draw the tree they picture in their imagination. Very rarely do they draw the root system, which actually is about half the tree, but unseen.

Trees as we know have extensive root systems which penetrate the earth where they take in the water and minerals they need to grow and survive.

You could argue that the roots are the most important part of the tree to its survival. If you think of the great Oak trees with their extensive root systems, you begin to get a picture of what it means to be grounded, to be rooted to the ground. This is an important aspect to meditation and sensory development work.

To be rooted, grounded also means to be connected. Like an electric circuit needs a wire called 'earth' to protect it. So do we need the grounding, earth, the rootedness to this earth we live on and love.

If we are not 'earthed', we can fly away, into our heads and consequently can become disconnected and even anxious.

But how do we reconnect to this earth, to this rooted, grounded way of being? Do we need to have our ' feet on the ground' to be grounded?

If you think of the woodsman in the forest, or the gardener or farmer, If you watch them at work they tend everything in a gentle, slow and methodical manner, there is no great rush or agitation. Quite the opposite to Wall Street or the city of London, which is fast, stressed and high octane.

Which would you consider more grounded?

I know the folks working with nature for me are often naturally grounded. I think it comes with working with the natural world; they quietly fall into its rhythms without even considering it.

But we cannot all give up our jobs and work with nature. We need to bring nature with us as we are nature, we are a part of nature and the more we reconnect with nature the more naturally grounded we are.

But until we have been practicing these techniques for a while, we need to learn a few tricks.

Can we feel grounded whilst in the crazy city, surrounded by sensory overload and fast living?

The first thing is to recall what we talked about in chapter 3 timing and tempo. If we just slow down just a tiny bit, say walk slower, think slower and relax a little, our energy literally feels like it drops back into our body.

Other tricks are finding time to be in nature, to attend to the garden is wonderful for grounding.

We can start to ground by focusing our energy away from our head; a foot massage is wonderful for grounding.

Dancing I find an excellent way to reconnect with the earth, by moving our 'but' on the dance floor we naturally ground and relax, and have fun!

Standing practices naturally connect us with the earth as gravity helps us connect! Let us explore a few 'Grounding practices'.

Practice 10

Grounding

The perfect place to practice this is of course in a quiet garden, standing in close proximity to a tree. But actually you can do this anywhere anytime.

You can do this practice sitting but I think it is easier from a standing posture.

Stand comfortably with your feet shoulder width apart.

Just drop your knees a little so they are in line with your toes. If that is uncomfortable do not worry, stand straight or sit down.

Allow your arms just to hang, relaxed by your sides.

Let you chest drop a little and relax.

Start by bringing your attention to your feet. The bottom of your midfoot is perfect. Can you feel the sock you are wearing?

Ideally this practice is done outside in a warm spot with no shoes and sock on, but you can do it just as easy with shoes and socks on.

Once you can feel the feeling of the sock, allow your attention to expand to feel your shoes- we can all do this. It is like how we can feel the road surface if bumpy when not touching it whilst driving. This sense of proprioception is totally normal to us- we use it all the time without even considering it.

Now feel the earth you are standing on.

Is it a soft carpet, a wooden floor, concrete, or soft grass? Can you feel it?

Now expand your attention a little further- send it about 6 inches into the ground and immediately you will feel a connection, it almost feels as if you strengthen in your center of gravity. It feels good.

It is as if the earth comes up to meet you.

This is harder to do if you are not on the ground floor but it is possible higher- you just have to 'send your attention deeper till it hits the ground.

Now be careful if you feel a little dizzy, this 'earthing' can drop your blood pressure a little, so go gentle if prone to low blood pressure. But conversely- do this a lot if prone to high blood pressure- it is good for you!

Just relax into the feeling of being connected to the earth around you, it feels a wonderful and totally natural way to be.

If you spend a few minutes sensing the earth, you can expand your attention all around to the earth as a whole, feel yourself connected to the planet as a whole. This can be difficult at first but sometimes the sense of the earth as a whole will come to you naturally.

Now if you are feeling agitated, ungrounded, and irritable, just try this practice for a couple of minutes and you will find it calming, grounding and relaxing.

Chapter 11

The Flow

'Life is a series of natural and spontaneous changes. Don't resist them; that only creates sorrow. Let reality be reality. Let things flow naturally in whatever way they like.'
Lao Tzu, **Tao Te Ching**

'Nature does not hurry, yet everything is accomplished.'
Lao Tzu

Laozi (or Lao Tzu) was a mysterious figure. The name literally means *old master*. He is known to be the reputed author of the Tao Te Ching and founder of Taoism (pronounced Daoism). He is a mysterious figure partly because it has been debated whether he even existed in some academic circles. It is widely thought that he lived in 6th century BCE in China.

It is told that, at eighty years of age, Laozi grew tired of the excesses of normal life. He went and lived as a hermit at the western gate of the city of Chengzhou. The sentry on the gate listened to his wise words and encouraged him to write a book.

This is reputedly the story of the birth of the famous works called the Tao Te Ching. The guard was so impressed with the old man's view of the world that he left his post and became his first disciple. Other stories about Lao Tzu include one that he travelled to India and became a teacher to Siddartha Gautama, the Buddha.

The **Tao** according to Taoism is the source of everything. It describes the unmanifest nature from which everything arises. Taoism calls for its students to return to a natural state, in harmony with the Tao - to be in the *natural flow of life*.

The concept of **Wu Wei** lies at the heart of the teachings. Wu Wei is non-action, or not-forcing, or *flowing with the moment*. This implies that to **be** with the Tao - the very nature of things - we need to be in a flow, like swimming in a flowing river. We either relax and flow downstream or we try to head upstream - against the flow - which is exhausting and difficult.

Going with the flow seems to be the simplest advice in the world, but how often do we do it? More often, we are disconnected from knowing where the flow is. We tend to apply concepts and thinking and drive ourselves on in our lives without even sensing the natural flow of things and without even knowing how to feel the flow. This makes life difficult for us.

If we could start to become aware of the metaphorical river we are in, then we could become aware of the flow. We could try to go with the flow and life could become easier and less tiring.

But how on earth do we go about finding the flow of things? Maybe, to start with, we can try to let go of any concept of destination. If we step off the bank in a metaphorical river, we enter the natural flow of it. We cannot decide to flow upriver if the flow is down. We must just step in and go with it.

Our problem is that mostly we want to go the opposite way. We want to fight the flow, so we employ thinking and concepts and get stuck in the state of going against things. This is exhausting, although on very rare occasions It may be necessary.

We must let go of this idea of going against the flow. To try to do that, what if we just take that first step into the flow of the river and see where it takes us. It would certainly be less tiring!

> *'A good traveller has no fixed plans and is not intent on arriving.'* **Lao Tzu**

Sometimes life grabs us and takes us in a direction which is beyond our control. It is like we are stepping into a very fast-flowing river. In this instance, we have no option but to go with the current or we will drown.

The difficulty of allowing ourselves to go with the flow arises when the flow is gentle, and we feel we can go either way. In this situation, it isn't obvious enough for us to know which way the flow is going. Sometimes, the object or goal is visible upstream just a bit and we try to swim against the current. But it tires us, and we get nowhere. We all know that feeling! But if we just hop in and relax, there may be a far greater goal around the next bend which was just beyond our vision on the bank.

> *'When I let go of who I am, I become what I might be.'* **Lao Tzu**

It seems that, to be in the flow of things or in The Tao, we first need a quiet mind. If there is too much noise, how can we sense anything? Going with the flow also implies that we can see beyond ourselves, that we can sense the bigger flow in the things around us. This implies that we are paying attention to what is around us.

Many indigenous tribes of the world paid attention to signs in nature and learnt to read them. The Bushmen of the Kalahari, the Australian Aborigines and the Native Americans could all see and track signs in nature for many uses. They could use signs in nature to read weather patterns, for tracking animals, and for following *songlines* (ancestral pathways).

In our modern, western lives, we have lost a great deal of that contact with nature. Our lives are more complex and there is an overstimulation of the senses. With this complexity, how can we read the subtle signs around us? There are always signs around us. Whether it is the subtle change in mood of a friend, or a certain action that we are trying to carry out that is proving tricky, or the change in air pressure preceding a storm. All these signs can tell us something if we take the time and effort to stop and look.

Why then, instead of thinking things out, don't we try to **feel** things out a bit? Next time you are unsure about a decision, ask yourself 'am I going with the **flow** here?" Or what **is** the flow here?

We have lost that direct rapport with nature and our own perception of what is obvious to do. Instead, we have learnt to apply logic. This works up to a point, but it does not stop us from swimming upstream most of our lives. And, as we have said before, this is exhausting and stressful.

Going with the flow doesn't mean avoiding responsibilities and not facing up to reality. Laozu spent a lot of time talking about social responsibility and leadership, about taking responsibility for community and country. The early Taoists would not spend much time in temples, preferring to be immersed in culture and community. From the midst of community, they taught of entering a place of Stillness from which choice could be clearly made.

To go with this deeper flow in life, this underlying nature of things, we need greater self-awareness, and to develop this greater self-awareness we need the courage to face our fears and to let ourselves be free to be moved by the tide of life.

To reconnect with the natural great flow of life, it could be suggested that we need three things:

1) To find a sense of quiet in our minds, a degree of neutral - a quiet stillness

2) To reconnect with nature and the natural tides in nature (which we will start to do next chapter).

3) To face our fears and emotions through the practicing of acceptance, allowing and observing (which we began trying in an earlier chapter).

We will return to Taoist practices of meditation, and internal alchemy, one of the roots of this practice, later.

Contemplation 11

Going with the Flow

First, let's apply what we already know about quietening our minds:

1. *We need awareness, a sense of being in our body. This we can do by tuning into our breathing, but with no judgement. We can also do this by feeling something delicate and soft in our breath, with any part of the body or the whole body. What we are doing is bringing our awareness, and our energy, back into our body.*

2. *The next important step is to apply acceptance, allowing and observing. It doesn't matter if we are stressed, if we are in pain or not, just allow and accept whatever state you are in. By doing that it starts to soften, like magic.*

3. *Things are now, I hope, starting to become quiet, fluid and open. From here, let's get a sense of our surroundings. We live in a fluid world - air is fluid, our bodies are like bags of fluid. Try to feel this sense of*

fluidity as we did in the last Practice. Everything is fluid. What does fluid feel like? Maybe a trickling, soft warmth or a sense of a babbling stream softly flowing or just the feeling of a liquid.

4. *Now try to open your awareness to the space around you, in the room or in the natural world around you. Use your feeling sense to try and notice a soft fluidity in nature around you. The natural world has many tides which we will start to explore in the coming chapters. For now, let's just open our awareness to our surroundings and be open to a sense of fluidity in things.*

As you sit quietly in this fluid world just open your awareness to potential movements within this fluid world which is all around us with its natural ebbs and flows. Let this fluidity hold your body and support it. Let the air around you act like a fluid. Wait there until this fluidity moves you into action - be it to go to the loo or get some food or whatever the moment requires.

Here we have started to explore the idea that we live in a potentially fluid world. If we step into our metaphorical river the current can take us. This implores trusting something outside ourselves and outside of our thinking world. Let's do this gradually. It is a big step if we are unused to trusting life and it can bring up emotions. If it does, apply the three tenets of acceptance: that you can have the emotion, allow the emotion and start to observe it and not be owned by it.

We will build on this next by looking more specifically at the fluid fields around us, and the Great Tides in nature.

Chapter 12

Our Fluid Body

"Nothing in the world is as soft and yielding as water
Yet for dissolving the hard and inflexible nothing can surpass it
The soft overcomes the hard
The gentle overcomes the ridged
Everyone knows this is true
But few can put it into practice.'
Tao Te Ching

The word *fluid* is defined in the Oxford English dictionary as 'something whose particles can move about with freedom, are able to flow and not ridged'. It is linked to the word flow, which can be defined as 'to move freely and smoothly'.

Our bodies are 90% fluid, of which 70% is water. It is amazing we can stand up at all! Some of the latest research in the development of embryos suggests that we could develop and form as groups of fluid fields, or different fluid massess. These fields of fluid slowly move and interact with one another. As they move and interact, it has the effect of changing the fields and even the cells which go on to start to form tissue. The groups of forming cells then come together, forming structures and starting to function as vessels, organs, the brain and so on.

In my work as an osteopath, we learn to feel and sense function in the body, from joint movements to more subtle fluid motion. We try to feel the gentle expression and breathing of fluid fields in the body. As a person's body relaxes they seem to become more fluid.

Our language reflects this idea of fluidity. For example, we talk of people relaxing and becoming more fluid, taking on less fixed and more fluid viewpoints. Here, fluidity implies more freedom, a softening and an ease.

When we strain a muscle or a joint, the process of inflammation and repair has an effect of creating hard, fibrous solid tissue within the damaged tissues. This is not a permanent thing. It is part of the healing process. At a later stage, this hardness starts to soften again. The hard, fibrous tissue is reabsorbed by the body and things start to soften and become fluid-like again as healing nears completion.

The problem often comes when the localized tissue damage remains and cannot go through the final stage of softening back to normal. That is when things can get stuck and symptoms continue longer than they should. As osteopaths, we find these areas of hard tissue and, using gentle manipulative techniques, act to restore a degree of fluidity to the local tissues.

Daoism philosophy talks about fluidity and softness, the softness and yielding water overcoming even the solidity of rock. The gentle fluidity of water running in a stream over many years can wear away the toughest rock formations and create deep valleys.

When our lives undergo a big change - like a change in career, relationship or loss of a loved one - if we remain fixed in old ways of thinking, the pain can go on longer than it should. If we remain fluid in our thinking, there is a good chance that we can adapt to the new circumstance quicker and easier.

When trained ballet dancers move, they seem to do so with such fluidity of movement, as if they are floating fluidly in space without the exertion that non-dancers must. It seems they are acting not as a fixed structure but as a fluid function. They flow.

Have you seen footage of the ease and fluidity with which a cheetah runs? It is fluid and effortless.

Our perception of our own body is not that of fluidity but of rigid bone structures holding us up. We are highly aware of areas of our body when they are blocked or in pain. These areas do not feel at all fluid - quite the opposite! If we could start to be able to sense a degree of fluidity within our body, it can help us to relax a little and change our awareness from what feels blocked to what feels fluid and even healthy.

Our body really is like a big bag of fluid, with its natural tides and flows. If we can start to sense a degree of fluidity in our body, then it may help us to find a degree of fluidity in our minds and thinking.

If we start to soften a little in our perception of ourselves and others, it seems to have the effect of letting things breathe a little. In western culture, the idea of yielding is connected with lack of strength. This may not necessarily be true. It may do the opposite. It may fix us in a position and in doing so it may have a blocking effect on us.

Fluidity can also mean strength, just as the fluid movement of water will eventually wear away rock. If we can start to build a deepening relationship with our own internal fluidity, it can lead to a general softening in our self-perception. It can start us on the process of feeling our internal self-correcting processes which keep us healthy and balanced.

As with everything we have done so far, we are in a process of developing our sensory awareness. This is a process that needs practice, or as the Daoists would say *cultivation*. We plant the seed and our developing practice is the cultivation process. The results will come with time and steady work, so here we will try to sense and feel our fluid body.

Contemplation 12

Sensing Our Fluid Body

Let's start by spending a few minutes getting a sense of the softness in our breathing. Remember to fully allow whatever thought or feeling that arises and gently bring back your awareness to the delicacy, softness, even fluidity in your breath.

Once you start to relax and feel somewhat neutral, open your awareness to your whole body. First, feel areas in it which feel tight and stiff. Just let your awareness be very light and fluid, let it move freely and not focus on one point or problem. Now, change your focus completely. Ttry to get a sense of something in your body that feels fluid, again just the tiniest, most delicate fluidity. If this is hard, try to sense a part of you that feels ok, happy, light. If you are in pain, try and focus on the part of you that is not.

Usually, when we start to feel this tiny fluid movement, it is fleeting - a microsecond of something which disappears and then can reappear somewhere else. This is what we are looking for. What we would call Potency in the body. If you look too closely it disappears, so maintain a very light, almost soft focus. If your perception becomes too focused and rigied and you employ thinking too much, you will lose it. This is purely a perceptual, feeling thing. If you cannot feel this, then bring your awareness back to the softness in your breath and stay with that for a few moments [and then try again].

Usually, at the beginning, you will only be able to feel this fluidity for short periods. As your practice deepens, you will be able to start to feel this beautiful fluidity in more and more of your body and eventually you will get a sense that your whole body is fluid. As we develop our practice, we will go on to feel our body as one drop of fluid. This fluidity in the parts will eventually become a whole fluid body acting as one. This brings a sense of wholeness and harmony and even peacefulness. This perceptual skill takes time to develop and we must go through stages in our perception and feeling.

The important thing here is to practice the steps, allow accept, observe any difficulties you are having. Don't get bogged down and do not think, this is purely a feeling process.

This sense of fluidity you are starting to feel is very important in the later steps where we can engage this to practice some self-healing techniques. The fluidity we are feeling here is an expression of the potency for health - the self-healing process in our bodies.

Chapter 13

The Fluid Fields In and

Around Us

'Each type of natural system has its own kind of field: there is an insulin field, a beech tree field, a swallow field etc. These fields shape all the different kinds of atoms, molecules, crystals, living organisms, societies, customs, even habits of mind'.
Rupert Sheldrake, Morphic Resonance and the Habits of Nature

Biologist Rupert Sheldrake caused a stir in the 1980s when he suggested that memory is inherent in nature. He suggested that the so-called laws of nature are more like habits and that nature's memory depends on a process which he called *morphic resonance.*

His work suggested that we live within energetic fields which have a collective memory - like a blueprint that in turn **forms us**.

A theory called *causative formation*. These fields have a memory of what it is like to be human, from the atomic, molecular level to that of cultural and collective memory and behaviour.

This work has resonances in other fields of science. In embryology, there is a growing popularity in the concept that we form as a system of fluid fields, which move and interact and relate, and through this motion and relationship **create** the perfect embryo form within it.

> *'The place of the embryonic formative process is a field (in the usage of the physicists) the boundaries of which, in general, do not coincide with those of the embryo but surpass them. Embryogenesis in other words comes to pass inside these fields. Thus, we have the visible embryo within its formative field.'*
> **Alexander Gurwitsch, 1922**

I have been teaching embryology to osteopaths internationally for many years now. How we form is so important to the structure and function of our bodies. We teach osteopaths to feel the remnants of these fluid forces which, having formed us, help to maintain the perfect blueprint for health.

Cell biology and the areas of epigenetic have echoed these views postulating the powerful effect of the fluid fields in the local and wider environment. These fields seem to have a role in the activation of specific genes. Scientists who work with the *new biology* are starting to think that the genes themselves are not the primary factor in our development. It is more the bioelectric fluid fields and local environmental micro-factors the genes are in contact with. Stem cells, which are precursor cells in the body are the same, but differentiate into vastly different cells, for example bone, liver or fat, depending on their location and immediate environment.

Sheldrake describes fields as *non-material regions of influence.* An example of this is the earth's gravitational field which is all around us and works through us, but we cannot see it. The moon moves around the earth due to the curve in the earth's gravitational field, and without it we would all float away.

Electromagnetic fields integrate all physical systems, from atoms to galaxies. For example, we can see this book because we are connected to it through an electromagnetic field in which the vibratory energy of light is travelling. Vibrating electromagnetic fields underlie the function of our brains and whole bodies, from cellular level to whole systems.

All around us there are countless vibratory patterns of activity within electromagnetic fields most of which we cannot detect with our senses. Some of these fields we tune into with our phones, radios and TVs, the process of tuning in is called *resonance*, where we move the dial to a point where the conductor - be it a radio or a phone - can be made to vibrate at a similar frequency as the radio frequency. This resonance allows the sound to be transmitted.

In addition to these larger wavelength fields there are countless other tiny fields - electron and neutron fields, and microscopic fields – in which all the particles of matter exist as tiny quanta of vibrational energy.

When our body forms, our heart starts to develop at the same time as blood, so it all begins with a flow. The flow of the fluid starting to move as blood about which form tubes and vessels which fold, rotate in relation to the flow direction needed, this in turn starts to form the heart.

The key point for us here is that these fields come first. They create the universe with all its structure and function. We are indeed a field, fluid body, which is constantly interacting with other fields, creating all aspects of life.

Michael Faraday, an English physicist from the early nineteenth century, was the first to theorize about fields. He discovered magnetism by witnessing the lines of force around a magnet. He saw that tiny iron filings placed around a magnet form ordered lines, showing the shape of the electromagnetic field. This is an experiment all children do early on at school.

Modern physics has really developed our thinking regarding the importance of viewing life as fields. Albert Einstein thought that fields could not be explained in terms of matter, rather that matter could be explained in terms of energy within fields.

From the wider planetary thinking of relativity, to gravitational fields, the effects on planets and stars, to the tiny fields within electrons, to the micro fields within which all particles of matter exist as quanta or packets of vibratory energy, everything be seen as a field.

Physicists for many years have been trying to link all these fields up, to find a unified original field of the cosmos, but thus far have been unable to do so. The closest scientists have come are the M- and string theory in which the maths adds up correctly. In these theories, we need eleven or so dimensions to make it work. We understand so little of the ideas of time and space.

The fields of biology and chemistry are only starting to catch up in the areas of epigenetics and the understanding of protein-folding and crystallization.

David Bohm reached an explanation of how these fields link together with his idea of *implicate order* in which he explains everything as a total wholeness in which everything is enfolding, so space and time are not separate. In this he sees everything, the multiverse, as a totality of flowing movement enfolding and unfolding again and again. This idea could explain the unanswered questions of quantum physics and field theories.

Rupert Sheldrake in his theory of morphic resonance talks about everything as a field, from memory, to instincts, to even insulin and other chemical compounds.

Relational fields and constellation therapies work by setting up family constellation fields. They utilize the memory of a specific emotional issue. By engaging with the field of this, by placing people in certain spatial relations in the constellational field, the participant can feel strong emotional reactions and releases when in fact they have never met the person concerned. I have witnessed this process myself and it is amazing.

The nature of fields of every kind is to be fluid, to be free to move and relate. If we start to change our thinking from the world being a solid structure to ourselves and everything being made of inter- relating fluid fields it will help us in our process of developing towards Dynamic Stillness.

In the course that relates to this book, I usually take the participants outside into nature and get them to start to feel these natural fields all around us. In our contemplation, I will introduce some of these fields.

Contemplation 13

Fluid Fields Around Us

For this exercise, we need to be outside in nature, ideally in a garden or wild space with plants and trees. But, if not, we can do this with any living thing, be it another person or an animal. Inanimate objects like rocks and crystals are possible to use but, at the beginning, it is harder to detect the fluid fields.

An ideal start would be standing next to a tree. Feel the bark with your hands and wrap your arms around the tree as much as you can. Try to get a sense of fluid movement inside the tree. Are there fluids, especially water, moving up the tree? Can you sense fluid movement under the hardness of the wood? Can you sense the lightest trickle?

If you don't feel anything, do not worry. If you think you can but are unsure if you are really feeling it, put it aside. We are just tuning in our senses to the potential of fluid. Our senses have much deeper and wider perception than we use, and we are going to start to broaden and deepen our feeling sense, this sense we can use through our pressure and touch receptors in our skin. We are going to deepen that, bringing in other sensory systems like proprioception – sensing ourselves in space, and what I call visual feeling – a sense that is on the edge of seeing but it is really a mixture of seeing and feeling. I will develop this idea as we go on with our work.

For now, just put out your hands in front of you and start to take a few steps backwards. What you are trying to feel here is the edge of the tree's field. This is felt as a subtle change in pressure on your hands. As you walk back - about one or two metres or more, depending on the size of the tree - you will start to feel a distinct boundary, the edge of the tree's field. When you sense this, just move backwards and forwards a bit to familiarize yourself with the edges of the field. If you have gone too far out and did not feel this subtle change in pressure, move slowly back towards the tree and see if you can detect any subtle pressure change in the air.

Remember, this is a very subtle pressure change and is new to our senses. Do not think about it too much - thinking blocks feeling!

If you do not get it straight away, try it again with a plant whose field is smaller and closer. If you are finding this difficult, then sit down and tune in to the softness of your breath. Allow, accept, then observe feelings and start to see it you can feel something soft, fluid and delicate inside your body. When you are in neutral, get up again and try once more to feel the tree field.

Once your senses are tuned into feeling these fields, it becomes easy. You can start detecting the fields in which all living things live within, from your pet dog to your partner or child. Once you can do this, start to detect the fields around inanimate objects, rocks, the sea or a lake. This should open a whole new sensory world to you.

Everything has a field, even the laptop I am writing on. As we sense these fields more and more, we begin to sense information in these fields. For example, if a child is unwell, their field differs. From this, we start to see that we are in a sea of connecting fields, which are constantly in communication.

This sensory awareness can be helpful if we are the type of person who can be sensitive and can react to people and places around us without knowing what happened. Those times when you enter a room and start to feel sad, or when you are close to someone on the train and start to feel angry for no reason. If we are aware of that and can sense it, we can choose to not react by feeling what energy belongs to us, and what does not.

So, developing sensory awareness is, in my view, helpful in having better boundaries and not being affected by other people and places. The wonderful thing to realize as we start to see and feel fluid fields is that they are fluid - meaning uncontained, with no tension - and is free to move. This perception is very important, and we will develop this practice further.

Chapter 14

The Story on the Wind

> 'Nothing is more common to the diverse indigenous cultures of the earth than a recognition of the air, the wind and the breath as aspects of a singularly sacred power.'
> **David Abrams, Spell of the Sensuous**

The word *Psyche* comes from the Greek for breath or gust of wind. The word *spirit* comes from the Latin *spiritus*, which again signified both breath and wind. Until the time of Socrates and Plato, the winds and air were seen by all cultures as sacred elements connecting all of us, including nature with its mountains, seas, animals and plants.

The Greek philosophers sought to change the emphasis more to a person-centered view of the world. Judeo-Christian philosophy focused on God being outside and above us, creating but not necessarily within nature.

The indigenous tribes sensed that awareness was not incorporated within a person, rather, it was carried on the winds and connected us all.

Socratic thinking brought this sense of awareness and the idea of psyche into and inside the realm of the body. Christianity has firmly sought to externalize God as a power not within and around us all and in nature, but otherworldly and separate.

The Navajo believe that wind is present in a person from the moment of conception, when two winds, one from each parent form a single Wind within the embryo. They say it is the motion of the Wind within the growing embryo or foetus that produces growth and development. They believe that when the infants are born this internal wind links with an external wind, which surrounds and enters them. The wind that surrounds them, they believe, grants life, movement, speech and awareness and connects all beings. It is thought to act as the means of communication between all things in the animate world.

Laurens Van der Post did a lot to document the ways of the Bushmen of the Kalahari. He was brought up at the turn of the twentieth century on a large farm on the borders of the Kalahari Desert in Africa. He spent many years, since his earliest memories, surrounded by what he called the *funny little people*, the Bushmen. These people were quite unlike other African peoples. They were small in stature, lighter skinned, with almost indigenous features. They lived a life always on the move and were amazing hunters. Laurens grew up with them and spent many years in their company, hunting and farming.

He has written many books about the Bushmen of the Kalahari, including The Heart of the Hunter and The Lost Tribes of the Kalahari, documenting their amazing ways. They are one of the original, timeless tribes of Africa who are lamenting the loss of their ways of living and their incredible art. These tribes became persecuted by the newer tribes in Africa, and their freedom to hunt and live a nomadic life was curtailed by land ownership.

In his books, Laurens tells stories about their incredible sensory perception of nature. They could sense a wild animal many miles away on the plains, they talked about the stories coming to them *on the wind*. This incredible perceptual awareness would bring with it a deep instinctual knowledge of the nature around them. This knowledge helped them to live for months hunting wild animals and finding water in the Kalahari Desert.

This awareness was starkly contrasted when Laurens would enter a town with them. They lost all their instincts and would be very uncomfortable and irritable. They would say that they had lost connection with the wind and would need to drink alcohol to cope. But when the Bushmen left the town they would soften, calm and would be visibly restored as soon as they felt the wind. What is that wind that connected them to nature and themselves and brought immediate calm and peace?

This story is repeated in other indigenous peoples. I lived for six months with the Mayans in Guatemala, treating them and learning their ways. They talked of a loss in connection to the nature around them, through exploitation and political upheaval, which caused distrust and disharmony within tribes and even families. I treated people still shocked and traumatized from the war, displaying a wide variety of symptoms.

William Sutherland, one of the earliest osteopaths working at the beginning of the twentieth century, would work on patients with gentle hands-on techniques. Sometimes, he noticed at certain times in the treatments, the room would quieten. A deep sense of stillness would be present and from the stillness this gentle, quiet, fluid tide, not water but fluid in its feeling, would enter the room. This sensation would infuse the patient and practitioner and the room, and the treatment process seemed to improve.

This slow, fluid motion has been termed the Great or Long Tide.

This movement is so natural and peaceful that both practitioner and patient would be able to feel it. It is possible for anyone to sense this. A delicate fluidity seems to be sensed on the edge of our perception. When we feel this Great Tide, it feels wonderful. It seems to connect us all. It seems very healing and calming in quality and it feels like we are deeply connected with nature.

When teaching students on the course to feel this Great Tide, everyone could feel it, but there seem to be certain prerequisites. Firstly, it seems that we need to be in a place of quiet neutral, where our nervous systems are not in overdrive and we are calm. Next, we need to try to open our awareness to the stillness behind everything as we did in the previous chapters. From here there seem to be a couple of steps which we can take to start to sense this Great Tide.

The Tide feels like the most natural thing in the world and feels amazing to sense. It seems that we start to feel almost *breathed by* life. We can relax and literally *go with the flow*. Going with the flow is, in my opinion, borne from being connected to the Tide. It is a state where we are not being driven by the workings of our psyche, but a slower natural and more instinctual force. This could be what Daoists call *being with the Dao*. We will develop our thinking on the Great Tide in the next chapter.

In my view, what we call the Tide is like the Wind of the Bushmen of the Kalahari and the Navajo. It seems like a wind that can connect and inform us, seeming to deepen our connection to our health and nature around us. It can potentially connect us with more instinctual elements within ourselves, bringing us a quality of peace and calm.

Contemplation 14

The Bigger Breath

[The Story on the Wind]

Sit comfortably and start to do the usual steps to bring a degree of neutrality to your nervous system. Practice the accepting, allowing then observing with thought, feelings and emotions. Bring your awareness to your breathing and do not judge it, just watch the breath as it enters and leaves your body.

After a few minutes you may start to feel a certain softness and warmth in your chest. Allow that feeling and just broaden your awareness to the movement of the breath. As you breathe in and out, really sense the feeling of the air as it hits your nostrils and your trachea and your lungs - this is an amazing feeling isn't it? You are sensing something that cannot be seen, yet it gives us life and is connected to everything else on this earth.

The Lakota tribes would smoke the pipe to see the movements of the air in the smoke and to sense the connection between each person and the surrounding air and winds. We don't need to smoke to sense this connection. There is a unified connection between us and everything. We are sensing that in our bodies.

Now, bring your attention to your skin. See if you can sense the weight of the air on your skin. It's a subtle feeling, but once you tune in, you can feel it.

We are surrounded by this air and we breathe it. It connects us and holds us. Try now to sense a degree of stillness in the air around and within you. Try to bring your awareness to the stillness around you, the quiet in the air you are breathing. Open your awareness wider and try to sense this connecting air, if you can, as far as to the horizon around you. Let your feeling sense really open out and breathe.

As we do this and deepen and broaden our sensory awareness, we start to deepen our connection with the ever-present stillness in and around us and connecting us.

In the next chapter we will connect with the Great Tide.

Chapter 15

The Great Tide

A t the University of Pennsylvania in the 1950s, a botanist called William Sefritz recorded a wonderful video of a slime mould.

Slime mould is an undifferentiated fluid mass of protoplasm without cell membranes. The video shows a slow rhythmic motion of the mould breathing in and out in cycles of around 50 seconds. This breathing movement is visible.

This slow and gentle rhythm is one we can find elsewhere in nature and even within our bodies. One could perceive it as a slow fluid flow which originates from stillness which moves and *breathes* living forms. This slow cyclic rising and ebbing is like a slow tide, not normally visible except in the mould, but it is possible to learn to feel this in living things and between living things, like a slow fluid motion.

It seems easier to perceive this tidal movement when we are in nature, sitting quietly and when we are aware of a certain stillness in and around us. From that place, it is possible sometimes to perceive, just on the edge of our senses, this fluid, wind-like quality arising from the stillness at the horizon and moving slowly toward us. This is the Great Tide.

This Great Tide has been documented in many cultures. The Tibetan Buddhists call it The Unconditioned Winds of the Vital Forces. The Navajo call it the Nilch'I or Holy Wind. The Bushmen of the Kalahari call it The Story on the Wind. In Hebrew, it is called Ruach or the Breath of God.

But what is most interesting about this phenomenon is that it is perceivable in nature to all of us. If we quieten the noise in our minds just long enough, it can make itself evident to us. When we start to sense this rhythm, it can bring an amazing sense of connection with nature and we can feel that our senses are opening. Then we can gain a deeper rapport with the nature around us.

What is surprising is that when we connect to this Tide, we can feel more connected with animals and birds. They can sometimes seem less instinctually fearful of us and can interact more. This sounds far-fetched but really it does start to happen. Birds can fly closer and wild animals can come out of hiding. When we sense this field or tide, we can often get a strong sense of being held by life. There is a sense of deep support offered to us by the universe, a sense that our systems are more than just our psyche and physiology.

Within our bodies, the Tide can feel like it is healing the body, bringing about a sense of rebalancing and restoration. The interesting thing is you would think that we live within this Great Tide all the time. The reality is that nature does very much seem to be connected to this tide. It seems though that us humans become disconnected from it.

Children seem to maintain connection, but as we grow older this connection seems to wane. I do not know why but it may have something to do with its natural slow rhythm. The breathing motion of this fluid is quite slow, taking about ninety seconds to reach us from the horizon and return there. Maybe as we grow up, we speed up our natural rhythm and in doing so lose this connection, like the Bushmen losing their connection to the Wind when they entered the towns. I am not sure, but what we really want to concentrate on here is learning to feel this tide and reconnect with it, which feels like the most natural thing in the world.

One of the biggest inspirations in me writing this book is that about ten years ago I showed a lady on the Dynamics of Stillness course how to reconnect with the Tide. Once she had experienced the feeling of it she said that it wasn't just important to do this, it felt like everybody's birthright. That struck me and inspired me to continue sharing what I have learnt. The question is why did we lose contact with this most natural of phenomenon?

I think it also has a lot to do with our progressive loss of contact with nature. People who spend much time in nature can find it easier to perceive the Tide compared to city folk. It is possible that it comes down to there being far too much internal and external noise for us to sense freely - internal noise meaning constant mental activity and external noise meaning the constant bombardment of the senses by life. It is entirely possible to sense the Tide in a city, in a deeply noisy or irritating situation, but this needs practice. To begin with, it is much easier to sense in nature, and with a quiet mind.

Contemplation 15

The [Great] Long Tide

Ideally it is best to be in nature but, if you are in the city, try to position yourself, sitting, with a view of the horizon.

Firstly, try to access a little awareness of inner peace by trying to sense a degree of softness, fluidity and delicacy in your breathing. Allow your internal noise to quieten by not blocking it. Allow yourself to feel it, but gently bring your attention back to a sense of softness in your breath. Allow yourself to feel the sounds and smells around you. Let them come into your consciousness and then let them soften into the background.

When you feel that you have a degree of neutral, start by trying to get a sense of the stillness behind everything. Then let your attention slowly move out towards the horizon. Enjoy the sense that your awareness is at the horizon. Be fully aware of this.

From here, just let your attention slip over the horizon - beyond where you can see. This feels odd at first because when you do this you feel like you are losing something for a second. Do not worry, it will come back!

Then, just wait. Wait until you start to sense your attention being slowly returned to you. You could also sense a slow, mist-like fluid motion coming from the horizon towards you. You can't see it, but you can sense it coming. It takes a while to come - about a minute and a half. As it approaches you, it passes straight through you, undiminished, but you get a subtle difference in sensation. You get the sense of feeling connected and infused and informed by this Wind. It feels like it supports you and holds you and calms you. It feels wonderful!

Then the tide will retreat back to the horizon, again slowly, taking about fifty seconds. If you wait, it will return, in a slow never-ending rhythm. It feels like it connects you to everything living around you. This awareness is hard to achieve, and you may not get it first time. Just bring your awareness back to the softness in your breath, let your nervous system settle and gently try again. This feeling is very subtle, but in the end all students on the course feel it and they do so at the same moment.

What is this Long Tide? Is it that we connect more deeply with the natural flows in nature? It's hard to explain, but it is evident and feels very connecting and healing.

As you practice this more and more, you can start to sense the tide coming in at certain quiet moments in the day. It may happen when there is a natural stillpoint or break in the constant action, or when you are doing a repeated rhythmic activity like knitting or washing up. The sense that you feel is that a slow, fluid movement almost breathes you. It feels wonderful!

So, if you keep your senses aware and open to your surroundings and try to sense the stillness around you, you could connect more and more to the Great Tide and the amazing depth of riches it can bring.

Chapter 16

Letting Our Senses Breathe

Our senses are how we feel and interpret the world around us. They develop well before we are born. We are receiving touch, pressure, taste, visual, hearing and even some smell stimuli as soon as these sense organs develop as embryos. The wiring of our brains at the time is simplistic, - our senses are not we use them today - but they are developing and starting to function.

Young babies respond to pressure changes and sound *in utero*.

Touch

Recent research suggests that the parts of the brain that map out where we feel **touch** in the body produce a map which is formed by the embryo/foetus [while it is] feeling its environment. In newborn babies, this map is enhanced by early touch, the touch from mother, father or other caregivers.

Physical contact has been shown to be vital to growth and development - touch reduces the reactivity of the body's stress systems and improves cognitive, emotional and immune function.

I have spent many years treating orphans from Romania who after birth were left in cots with no physical contact. They would suffer [limited or slower rates of physical] growth, developmental delays and [diminished] immune and cognitive development.

[The sense of touch is important throughout our lives]. Embryos at five weeks can sense touch on their nose and lips, and by twelve weeks they can sense touch all over the body. A baby's first developed sense is touch. It is vital for bonding, for feeding and it aids brain development. A touch can be ultimately soothing, or it can be the opposite. As adults, if our touch sensors in the body receive constant stimulation, for example, say the pressure of our clothes on our body, the brain desensitizes to them, so we don't feel them as much.

The sensory map is at first diffuse but slowly it sharpens as the baby grows. As we grow this sensory map, it becomes sharply defined and has a close connection to our developing emotions.

Some people with sensory developmental differences can find difficulty in these areas. As a young child, my daughter could not wear socks - she found the ridges of the seams too irritating. I had to send off to America for seamless socks!

Our senses must desensitize us to certain stimuli. This is vital for life. Our senses become desensitized when they are over stimulated. Since we live in a world of sensory overstimulation, our sensory awareness shuts down as a natural coping mechanism.

Smell

Our ability to **smell** begins at around twenty-eight weeks *in utero*. The area of the brain that processes the sense of smell has a strong connection with the areas of the brain that focus on emotion and memory due to its location. Certain smells calm the foetus pre-birth. The smell of amniotic fluid has been shown to calm the baby in the womb.

The smell of the mother is important for a baby in bonding with his or her mother. It relates to a sense of nurture in our emotional makeup. Similarly, the smell of the father is linked to a sense of safety and comfort. Newborn babies can discriminate smells nearly as well as adults. However, their response is more direct - differing smells can directly affect their heart rate, breathing or aversion (turning away from a stimulus).

As we grow, our sense of smell links with certain deeply felt emotions and memories. A certain smell can bring back a distant memory or feeling. For example, the smell of a partner can affect us deeply. Women and girls have a stronger sense of this - testosterone in boys and men blocks this to a degree, it is possible that this harks back to male hunting days.

Our emotional experiences mean that we become conditioned to smells and, especially, we can become insensitive to some smells. Emotional stress can block our senses, especially the sense of smell.

This deep patterning of the sense of smell in our memory and deeper emotions can be important in developing ourselves in our Dynamic Stillness work as well as in developing our sensory awareness. Our sense of smell can be used to positive effect. Smell therapy and aromatherapy can have a direct effect on our emotions, bringing calm and a sense of peace.

Taste

Taste is a much simpler sense than smell. We can divide the sense of taste into four categories - bitter, sour, sweet and salty. Taste is highly dependent on our sense of smell - that is why, when we have a cold, food often tastes bland.

As we have found out with our sense of smell, taste also connects closely with our emotions. The taste of amniotic fluid calms newborn babies. Babies can decipher all four categories of taste, but they prefer the sweet taste to all the other taste sensations. Sweet flavour receptors in the brain release opiates directly into the blood stream, which is calming and bring pleasure. That is part of the reason why we like the taste of chocolate so much and explains why we tend to eat sweet things when we comfort eat.

Vision

Our sense of **vision** is still primitive at birth. It is less important in bonding than the senses of touch, smell and taste. But our visual pathways in the brain wire up very quickly. By six months of age, all our primary visual ability is in place: depth, colour, acuity and coordinated eye movement. Vision takes up more processing space in the brain than all our other senses put together.

As we grow our brains learn to discriminate visual stimuli to what is important and what is background. We respond to changes in our environments and block out constant stimuli. In some ways this is necessary, otherwise our nervous systems would be constantly overwhelmed by too much stimuli.

Hearing

This is also true of our sense of **hearing**. A foetus *in utero* can hear from around the age of twenty-three weeks. They hear their mother's voice and her heartbeat, and they can also discriminate other voices like that of their father and siblings *in utero*. This discrimination plays a role in language development. Babies have been shown to prefer certain books that have been read to them *in utero*, along with certain music.

From this, we see that our senses develop early and become the method by which we sense our immediate environments and form responses in behaviour and emotions. On a pre-conscious level, we are reacting all the time to these stimuli without even being aware of it.

Over a thousand years ago, the Daoist practitioners were aware of the importance of our senses and applied a variety of techniques to work with the senses, especially in meditation and alchemical working (we will talk in more detail about Daoist Alchemy in a later chapter).

In many Daoist meditation practices, the practitioners would start by *closing down* their senses. This process of closing down was almost a way of bringing their sensory awareness back into their bodies. The Daoists were interested in the way we *lose energy* via our senses. They maintained that in order to successfully meditate, it was important that they return their senses back into their body first.

In my work in teaching sensory development for practitioners,

I am more interested in becoming conscious of where our senses are, meaning becoming conscious of exactly where we place our attention within the moment.

If we can become conscious of our attention through our

senses, we can learn to shift our attention at will, learning to optimize sensory awareness as well as to develop levels of Stillness.

The senses are so important that I will come back to them in a later chapter and the topic is large enough that I will develop it into a book. The senses and developing a *felt sense* by specifically combining senses in different ways are fascinating.

For now, let us develop our practice with some sensory awareness practices.

Practice 16

Letting our Senses Breathe

As we progress here in our practice, it may seem like we go over and over the same old ground. There is a purpose to this. In my view we are looking for a real change in our practice, in our sensory awareness, in our relationship to ourselves and our Health and a deeper connection to the deep tides in nature. Also, we are developing a deepening relationship to Stillness and eventually Dynamic Stillness, and with it a deepening sense of wholeness and oneness. This is a huge task and takes time, like planting a seed and tending the growing sapling daily. This cultivation, in my experience, brings wonderful results, but there is no fast path to sustained growth. The tending must be constant and consistent.

Let us hope that the journey is fun too!

To begin this chapter's practice, sit comfortably. For this session, you can choose to be outdoors in nature or not. Either way, it is possible for your senses to be filled and emptied!

Bring your awareness to your breath and do not judge it, sense the stillness and quietness or the potential for them in your breath.

Once you start to feel a little neutral and calm, bring your awareness to your sense of touch. For this, let's focus on our palms. If they are facing down on your legs, turn them to face palms upwards, so they are not touching anything material.

Bring your awareness to the weight of the air on your hands. It becomes very real as we bring our attention to it. Enjoy the sense of the weight of the air on your palms and let your touch sense widen, as if you are holding up the air in the room. Can you feel that? It connects you to the room or, if you are outside, to the horizon.

From here, bring your awareness of touch back so that it feels like it returns to you, back inside your body, and again there is nothing to feel in your hands. What I am interested here in is developing our ability to move our sensory awareness or attention at will.

Let's try this again with our vision this time, for this it helps to have a horizon in view. Bring your visual awareness to your immediate surrounds and enjoy for a second what is around you. Then allow your visual awareness to move slowly to the horizon, as if you are allowing the visual sense to breathe out to the horizon. Now as we did with the Tide Practice before, let your visual awareness drop over the horizon and wait in comfort, knowing that it will return to you on the Great Tide.

Let's try this now with our hearing. Start by listening to the immediate sounds in your environment, the small sounds of your breathing, or the background noises in the room. Now let your hearing expand to outside. Really let the sense breathe out, like you almost feel you are] with your hearing the outside world. Now try to hear the Stillness that is behind the noise. Can you hear it? It is always there ...

Chapter 17

Nature and Connection

As we have seen in recent chapters, our world is made up from a huge variety of interacting fields and fluid tides. This is borne out both by modern science and the deep knowledge of the indigenous tribes of the world. It seems that our modern senses need to catch up with this understanding. Our practice is developing this, our sense awareness, with the hope that we will begin to start to sense these fields and tides, which can open us to a deeper world of connection and peace.

Over successive generations, through scientific discovery and agricultural and industrial revolutions, mankind has learnt to harness some of the elements in nature, to grow food to sustain the rapidly expanding population, to provide power to run our homes and businesses and to make medicines to stem disease and to build homes. In doing so, we have lost that deeper connection with the natural rhythms in nature.

In older times we would almost hibernate in winter, stock up harvests, create and sustain warmth and curtail activities as we endured the harshness of winter. The story is very different now. At our local supermarkets we can buy almost any food types at any time of the year, we can provide environments that feel like summer in midwinter and vice versa.

Through this dietary and environmental progression, we have lost contact with the natural rhythms and how they affect our bodies within the year. In my view, certain food types suit our bodies in differing seasons. For example, in summer, lighter foods, fruits and salads and uncooked foods suit us better. In winter, however, warm soups and broths serve us better. Nowadays, there are large fads for cold smoothies with raw veg and fruit in them at any time of year. This, in my view, overburdens that natural process in our digestive system, and cause digestive problems.

I am not romantically craving older days where there was no technology - I love technology! - but I think we need to remain connected to Nature's rhythms and tides, not only to maintain good health but to deepen the richness of our existence and become fully conscious of the harm brought by our loss of connection to the natural rhythms.

These ideas are not new. Every day, we hear from different sources that humans are destroying the earth. We become numb to these words, feeling that nothing can be done about Global Warming or the destruction of the world's coral reefs. We hope that nature will adapt, or future generations will discover new ways to ensure planetary survival. But is that enough?

In my view, the deeper we connect with nature, the more conscious we become. One of my hopes with these practices is for us to wake up to nature and live more symbiotically with it, not unconsciously try to harness and control it.

We find nature everywhere we are. I am always surprised to discover, when in central London, the number of foxes moving amongst us, even in Trafalgar Square! Wherever we are, we can find a minute to connect and enjoy nature.

Of course, it is best in the country, best of all in those rarified wildernesses that are barely touched by mankind, where the stillness can become deafening in its power.

I remember I would fly into London on a Thursday evening to my practice in Harley Street each Friday. When I got off the tube, I would sit on a wall under some magnolia trees, with London's busiest road just in front of me. I had come from the easy stillness of my practice in the countryside of rural Tipperary into the heart of London and the noise was overwhelming. But I would sit under those beautiful trees and acknowledge what an amazing job they did, right by the Westway in London, bringing beauty and stillness into the chaos.

I would sit there for half an hour in the late evening, ignored by the passersby - apart from the occasional tramp - and acclimatize to London, connecting to the underlying stillness behind all the noise. In the spring, the blossom on these trees was unsurpassed!

I want us, in this work, to start to build our connection with nature, so we can start to learn to read its patterns, stories and tides, not just for our sake but for all of nature - we are part of nature and we tend so easily to forget that.

Western belief systems have increased our disconnection from nature. Most of the world's religions have placed God as an outside force, which is different from the indigenous tribes of the earth, who always place god in everything and see us humans as part of an interconnected whole. This, coupled with our modern western reductionist philosophy, [which is based on rationality and logic rather than intuition serves to disconnect us further from feeling a strong, clear and consistent connection with nature.

This all makes it very hard for us to feel this deep connection with nature. Technology, sensory overstimulation and city life take us [even] further away. I am not saying that we should all start worshipping the earth, moon and stars as gods, but if we engage with the idea of accepting that everything is part of an interconnected One - which makes most sense to me, philosophically, scientifically and morally - it could help us to make that reconnection with nature. If we place ourselves as an integral part of nature, it helps us to find a deeper connection with what is around us. This also helps us to connect with our own nature, which is an expression of our Health.

Our practice here is to develop our connection to nature, through going through the stages we know already - allowing our senses to slowly expand, to start detecting Stillness in and around us, to start to feel Fluid Fields and Tides within and around us - and then to start to contact and connect with these fields in nature.

In some of the older Daoist teachings from nearly a thousand years ago, there are many practices for engaging with different elements in nature. There are some beautiful techniques for connecting with and melding with different elements in nature. At my practice in Tipperary, after work, I go into the courtyard and practice a variety of processes and practices that I have discovered through ancient books and teachings. These bring a sense of connection with nature.

There is something beautiful about standing in the stillness of the night and connecting with the energy of the moon, or first thing in the morning meeting the dawn sunrise or feeling the gentle fields of trees and plants. I always teach about these different examples of connection on the Dynamics of Stillness courses, allowing students to connect with the fields of trees and plants. Students really enjoy [feeling these connections]. The amazing thing is if we meet nature with respect and gentle awareness, it seems that nature engages back!

In 2001, I started to work with the natural energetics in plants in the form of making flower essences very much in the same way as Dr Bach [Dr Bach's Flower Remedies] started to do in the 1930s.

I have made more than eighty essences from separate flowers and thirty combination essences. The key to them is sensing them through their energetic fields and seeing how the flowers interact with the energy fields of a person. Usually, I would get my children to hold a flower and I would try to read its effects on their fluid fields. It sounds odd, but the flower essences really are wonderful! I call them the Irish Wildflower Essences, and I have been using them for over fifteen years now. They are available from my practice and they are gentle and supportive. I learned to work with these essences by becoming more able to perceive these fields in nature. Working with the flower essences helps me connect more deeply with nature.

Let's now develop our practice by letting our senses connect with those in nature.

Practice 17

Nature and Connection

For this practice we really need to be outside in nature, ideally in a garden or park. We are going to use a standing posture for this practice.

Stand, ideally within touching distance of a tree or flower or shrub. If it is warm enough, it is lovely to do this practice in bare feet.

Stand facing the plant or tree. Place tour feet shoulder width apart, knees just slightly bent, arms at the sides and your palms facing the ground.

Let your body relax into this standing posture. Feel your feet on the floor, bring your attention to the mid-foot, just behind the ball of the foot. This point is K1 (kidney 1 in Daoism/ Chinese Medicine). From here, expend your awareness about twelve inches into the ground below this point and start to sense your connection to the earth. This is a lovely technique to do if you feel you need to ground *yourself, to feel connected to the earth], or you have been doing a lot of work with your head/ brain, like studying. This brings you back into your body and **earths** you.*

We can repeat our usual practice of finding our neutral - by tuning into the softness of our breath, by accepting, allowing and finally just observing thoughts, feelings and emotions. Then, when you are comfortable and quiet, try to get a sense of the quiet stillness behind the sounds around you.

Next, I want you to start to sense a degree of fluidity within yourself - the sense that you are fluid. From this point, I want you to extend your arms to touch the tree or plant. Touch the tree softly, almost as if your hands were transparent and quiet. Try to sense fluidity with your hand. Is there any fluid movement up the tree? The process of transpiration usually means water is drawn up through the roots to the leaves of the tree. Can you feel this?

Next, try to take a step backwards so that your outstretched hands are about twelve inches from the tree. I want you to see if you can feel the trees field. There is a definite boundary to the field of the tree. The field of a plant is about twelve inches fully around it, but the field of a tree is much bigger - we are talking nearer three or four metres as the usual field boundary for a good-sized tree. Move back until you sense with your hands a change in density of the air around your hand. You will now be able to feel the boundary of the field of the tree. Repeat this with plants, rocks and other items in nature as we did in the chapter on fluid fields around us.

Now I want you to feel a sense of natural connection with the tree, as if there is a harmonizing of the fluid fields of you and of the tree. It's like you and the tree are hugging and meeting. It feels wonderful! Do you feel a deeper connection with the tree?

Chapter 18

Mastering Attention

As we go on developing our practices, we are learning some very specific skills. This skill base will continue to grow as we go through the coming practices.

One of the most important elements which we are learning is to firstly become aware of, then to master exactly where we place our attention at any given moment.

In the coming chapters we will learn to shift our attention at will. We have already started to learn to expand our attention to the Stillness around us, The Stillness on the horizon, and to sense Stillpoints within us and in the environment around us.

As we go on we will learn to place specific focused attention to elements within nature.

We will also start to learn to place our attention in particular ways *inside* our body, learning to shift our attention from what feels blocked in our body to what feels nice, and in doing that connect to the energy in our body which is working for it's Health. By tuning into this vital expression of Health, we go on to learn rudimentary healing techniques, both self healing and healing with others.

These steps allow us to focus and expand our attention. Also to allow our attention to be free, to flow with the natural flow and dynamic of life, and again to focus our attention when the timing is perfect for us to do so.

Here in our practice we are going to work to increase our attention on our attention, to become conscious of where our attention lies, moment to moment.

If we do this, the first thing it does is bring us directly into the moment.

For example when we become aware that our attention is on some past event or some future scenario, what happens?

The very action of being aware of our attention bring our attention directly back to the moment.- clever trick really and so simple!

If we play a little with our attention, let it just go wherever it wants in time and space, a happy time back in the past, in a specific place, with a specific loved one, it is like part of us returns to that time and place. If we are bring conscious awareness to that we remain connected to the moment.

This is an important element of developing a meditative practice, it does not matter where your mind goes, as long as we are conscious of it, we are brought back to the moment in a non-judgemental way and it actually feels good.

So the art of mastering our attention starts with becoming conscious *to* our attention, in a non judgemental manner.

Once we are conscious of our attention we can then decide what we want to do with it, we can learn to shift it at will.

My next book called 'The Anxiety Brakes' develops this idea. If we can learn to master our attention, we can learn to place it exactly where we want it in place, time and feeling. From this we can access a whole world of possible ways to stop the anxiety.

For us here, learning to become conscious of our attention, we can learn to shift it anywhere, anyplace anytime and to any though, idea, feeling and emotion we choose.

By maintaining consciousness of it we always keep one foot in the present as well.

The first step when becoming aware of our attention in the moment is to act softly. To soften our focus just a little, so our attention can feel free to roam, so we do not fix it down.

This again is important when stressed and anxious because when we feel that way the first thing we do is fix our attention, fixate on something- usually a negative thought, feeling or emotion.

So we actively soften our grip on our attention. How do we do that? We do that by actively softening our attention, our focus. Just allow it to soften with your mind- it works immediately when we try it usually. If not keep at it and allow all feelings that come up. If we practice the Acceptance, Allowing and finally observing that we learned early on in this book it immediately works to loosen our grip on our attention.

So once our attention is free we can learn to send it wherever we want, whenever we want, this is a wonderful experience once you practice it a little. It helps you connect very deeply with whatever you place your attention on, especially in nature.

Let's try to practice this a bit.

Practice 18

Mastering Attention

Find a comfortable spot, in nature is best, but a view would be ok. No view will work if that is where you are.

Sit comfortably and allow your breathing to soften just a little.

Now just become aware of where your attention is and allow it be there.

It could be with the work you were just doing, some worry with the kids, or it could be on a future or past event. It could be just on the garden outside or just on my words.

As you do this just try to soften your attention, so that it touches whatever it touches lightly, like a feather.

It really doesn't matter what you place your attention on at all- just accept, allow and observe and we have learnt to do.

Now, if you have a view outside, just let your attention go to something that draws you in your visual environment. As you do this remain conscious that you are placing your attention wherever you are.

Now place your attention on your hearing and let your hearing pick up whatever it can- still keeping totally conscious that you are placing you attention on your hearing.

Now place your attention on something positive from your past- a good memory, really allow your mind's eye to see that memory become aware of the sounds, smells and visuals, also the feelings in the memory, all the while maintaining consciousness, or awareness that you are doing this.

It's a funny little trick this, but serves an important purpose.

Now try the same - can you project your attention into the future- something that you are looking forwards to? Try to bring in the senses again, the visual, hearing and even smell of it, While you do this keep a little of your attention on the fact that you are doing this.

Do you get the picture? It's a really subtle thing, but by maintaining awareness of where your attention is, and keeping your attention light as a feather we can learn to become a master of our Attention whilst at the same time not fixing it down, allowing it to feel free, whilst learning to place it with precision wherever we wish it to be.

We are learning an important skill which we will develop as we go on.

Chapter 19

Alchemy

We have focused on fluidity, on fluid fields in and around us, on the great Tides of nature, the story on the wind and we have started to open our senses to this gentle fluid motion. This is a starting point in our sensory and perceptual development. From here, we are going to turn our awareness towards sensing where this motion arises. From here, we are going to try to feel the Stillness, be it in a place, location or perception.

Like many people, I have long been interested in the process of *alchemy*. Alchemy is a complex subject but at its core is the process of transformation, transmutation and transubstantiation, which is turning one form of matter into another like lead into gold.

Alchemy can be thought of both as a philosophy and a practice which can be looked at on many levels.

Alchemy is a process, which has been in the world for almost four thousand years. There are three main areas in which it grew up - in Daoist China, in India and in the West.

Western alchemy is thought to have come from Egypt, the city of Alexandria being the centre of alchemic knowledge. The term alchemy comes from the Greek word for Egypt.

From Egypt it travelled to the Islamic world, then finally to Europe.

The aims of alchemy have been two-fold. The first, the physical transmutation, is known as *exoteric alchemy* [*exo* means external and links to physical transformation]. This involved the purification and perfecting [the physical characteristics of certain objects – especially base metals – which could lead to, for example, turning lead into gold. Exoteric alchemy was also focused on creating an elixir of immortality, also called the *philosopher's stone.*

The second aspect of alchemy, *esoteric alchemy* [eso meaning internal] was more about an inner transmutation, [a transmutation] of the spirit, which again involved internal purification to a more enlightened state of being. In this case, the elixir was more internal.

Many historians think one form of alchemy cannot be separated from the other, even that the exoteric was a metaphor for an inner transformation.

Daoist Alchemy also had exoteric and esoteric aspects. Alchemy in China began more as a search to find and refine medicines but the exoteric alchemy was also concerned with refining base metals. Similar to western alchemy turning base metals into gold.

Daoist Esoteric alchemy concerned itself with inner transformation.

My understanding of Taoist esoteric alchemy comes from writings from the Song dynasty in the 14th century, notably from the schools of Complete Reality Daoism.

Daoist Esoteric alchemy consisted of three stages of transformation. The first stage was the ingesting of certain substances for the process of spiritual development. This typically involved the ingesting of Mercuric Sulphide, which was tolerable at low levels, but it was poisonous if too much was taken in one go.

Swallowing the poison at low levels was thought to help the practitioner to find deeper spiritual states.

The second level of Daoist esoteric work concerned itself with the internal transmutation of energy. Typically, this involved the process of tuning into different natural energies in the body and learning to move them. This process had been termed **Nei Dan**. For example, the *jing* energy, which has a concentration in the pelvis, is moved to the heart area where it is converted to *qi,* a lighter more refined energy. The next step is to move the qi energy to a place in the middle of the head where it is converted to *shen* energy, an even lighter, more spiritual energy.

What interests me here is the third process for esoteric, internal, alchemy as practiced by the Daoists of the some of the Complete Reality schools. The third process describes a somewhat deeper process, which links very much with our developing practice. It involves sitting in a meditative posture and finding the place where motion arises from stillness. In different texts, this can have a location, typically at a place just below the umbilicus - the *Dan Tien* - or in other texts it is described as a place behind the mid-brow. Other schools and masters would say there was no location for the *Dan Tien*, just a feeling sense quality.

In alchemical Daoism, the *Dan Tien*, this place or sensory experience, is called the *opening*, the place from which movement arises, where the manifest arises from the un-manifest. In Daoism, what they call the Dao is both the manifest and the unmanifest - they are all within the Dao - but an important part of Practice development in Daoism is to learn to wait at the opening, at this place from which movement arises.

For the Daoist practitioner, once you can learn to wait at this place in the body or have a sense of the feeling place, an opening occurs. This can give rise to the presence of a spiritual elixir, a quality of connection with something deeper and more connected, which is deeply peaceful and transformative. From this place, they say the *spiritual embryo* develops. This sense quality they say needs nurturing for a period, metaphorically nine months, the same amount of time needed for a new human to develop. This incubation or cultivation period needs to last until a deepening connection occurs.

Cultivation means practicing regularly. The more we practice it, the more we gain from it. Our practice deepens, bringing with a myriad of positive effects on our lives.

I find the practices of alchemy interesting. Throughout history, alchemy has been cloaked in mystery, with the practices protected by secrecy and symbolism. For me, though, the essential practices of inner transformation by cultivating a connection to Stillness is relevant, effective, and potentially fundamentally transformative, especially in the modern world.

These alchemical practices have a relevance to what we are doing in the Dynamics of Stillness. The process of cultivation means that by practicing techniques steadily and repeatedly, our practice deepens in many subtle ways. Firstly, the practice becomes easier to do. Then, as we practice, we can start to enter these states at will, more and more easily. This may seem a difficult jump in our practice, but we have put together already quite a strong armoury of skills.

We can by now bring our mind to a neutral place, we are starting to feel the tides in and around us and we have started to feel the Stillness behind everything. From here, we are going to put this all together and find the transition point between stillness and motion and try to maintain an awareness of this place or feeling.

This chapter's practice – can be achieved in many ways. I will mention two for now. The first is to develop our practice of connecting to the Great Tide by sending out our awareness to the horizon, as we did before in the chapter on the Great Tide. This time, though, we are allowing our awareness to rest lightly by waiting at the Stillness on the horizon, this time keeping a sense of awareness there, even when the Great Tide moves in and out. In doing this, we are splitting our awareness to feel both the slow tidal motion of the Long or Great Tide whilst simultaneously keeping an awareness on the Stillness at or beyond the horizon.

I am asking you to do something new here - this idea of splitting our attention. [If you think about it, though] this is something we do all the time. We can have an awareness of many things at once, like tasting food whilst hearing music. But here we are going to split our attention within the feeling, or sensing world, that we are developing.

I will elaborate on this in the Practice.

The second way is to sit quietly and to start to feel a degree of internal fluidity in or around yourself. It can be anywhere around you or inside you. From here, I want you to find the Stillness that is behind the motion and to again sense both Stillness and Fluidity at once. Once you can start to feel both, try to sense the place where Stillness meets motion, or the place where motion arises from Stillness. I often find this easier to do by sensing the underlying stillness that is everywhere including inside me whilst watching my internal fluid fields breathe. Then, sensing the place where they meet, or more accurately the place where motion arises from stillness.

I will develop this again in the two-part practice.

Practice 19

Finding the Point where Motion Arises from Stillness

Part 1

For this Practice we need a view towards a horizon, ideally in nature but any horizon will do. Start by sitting comfortably and going through the familiar process we know by now of finding neutral, allowing our brains to release their grip on our senses, so they are free to breathe.

When you are comfortable and calm, allow your visual awareness to slowly and naturally expand to the horizon and, as we did before, just let your awareness drop over the horizon.

Now from this place, open your feeling sense to the quality of Stillness that is present at the horizon or over the horizon. Just wait there and enjoy the sense of peace and stillness. Soon you should start to get a sense of the Tide moving very slowly like a quiet cloud from the horizon. From here, split your awareness so that part of you is watching the motion and part is with the stillness it comes from.

Part 2

For this you can be anywhere. Start by sitting comfortably and quietly and focus on the softness in your breath. By allowing, accepting and observing, your nervous system will naturally quieten to a feeling of neutral. From here, just allow your attention to be moved to something that feels fluid in your body. The fluidity is a freedom of motion and implies movement. All of your body acts like one unit of fluid, which is softly breathing in a gentle very slow rate. This is much slower than your respiratory breathing, more like two to three cycles per minute. It is a soft, gentle breathing which is already being expressed in each cell of your body.

*Now allow your awareness to take in the natural stillness that lies behind this fluid **breathing motion**. Can you sense both stillness and the fluid breathing at the same time, or the place where the fluid motion arises out of stillness? It is not in a location, it is a felt sense, a quality of feeling. If you don't feel it straightaway, you will soon.*

Chapter 20

Fulcrums

There are two definitions in English of the word *fulcrum*.
The first is from physics, which defines it as the point at
which something is balancing or is supported. The other is
more human from biology, sociology, psychology: it is defined
as the main thing or person needed to support something or
make it work or happen. For our purposes, both definitions are
relevant.

Fulcrums are things we can learn to feel with our developing
felt-sense. What I am interested in here is that we start to get a
felt-sense of fulcrums both in and around our bodies. When it
comes to fulcrums that we can feel around us, we need to start
to focus our senses - particularly our feeling sense that we have
been working with – and become aware of where it is in relation
to us – is it near or far.

I will give you an example of this. Every morning, when I wake
up, the first thing I do is sense my energy, and to feel if any of it
is not in me. Our energy can be dragged off in many directions
through thoughts, dreams, feelings and emotional connections.
Other factors can also affect the felt location of our energy. If

my feelings are with my partner or with my children and we are apart, it often draws my energy away from me, by becoming aware of where my energy is it naturally returns to me.

When I am teaching a course, the first thing I tend to do is to see if everybody has arrived. I am looking to see if their energy is with them, or if they are still partly with their families or the travelling or in their thinking. I literally, make sure they have completely arrived.

An interesting anecdote on this idea is when, in the 1950, a group of Native Americans flew by aeroplane to visit some dignitaries in London England. The 'plane arrived at Heathrow, but nobody moved a muscle. When asked why, they replied that they were waiting for their spirits to catch up! And sometimes it feels like this. Remember, we live in a quantum world where everything consists of packages of energy which resonate and relate to one another and where distance is irrelevant. If we think right now about a loved one, we send some energy toward them. If we have many things to think, worry and concern ourselves with, it can be very tiring!

I am suggesting here that we have fulcrums in and around us for a great many things. These fulcrums are balance points between ourselves and the object, person or thought in question. We can also send our energy back in time by engaging with a memory. Likewise, we can send our energy into the future by thinking about possible future events and ideas. Other factors can produce fulcrums that we can learn to feel in and around us and others.

When teaching osteopaths to develop their palpation and perception skills/awareness/practice. I teach them to start to feel these fulcrums in other people. They can affect the body by creating sensations of pulls and drags in and around the body.

A midline is a central fulcrum. This can act like a centre of gravity in the body. If a patient has suffered an accident or a shock they shift their entire midline to a new place. For example, if someone suffers a road traffic accident and is hit from behind, their midline fulcrum can move from inside the centre of their body to a place in front of them. The same thing happens with someone who is in shock.

A dramatic example of this happened while I was helping a colleague treat a patient. I knew nothing about the patient or his history, but I came in to help. As soon as I tuned in to him, we both could see a strong fulcrum/midline down to the side of the plinth he was lying on. We both acknowledged it and then something dramatic happened. The patient nearly fell off the table and then acted as if passing out. He slowly came around and my friend put a blanket round him.

When he had recovered, the patient told us his story. He was a coffee producer from Africa. One day he had an accident in his jeep. The jeep had veered off the road and turned over going down a steep embankment. He had woken up in a hospital. This accident had created a shock and moved his midline fulcrum.

The amazing thing was, as he came too, he said, "I'm feeling completely different." All his pains, in his head, neck and back had immediately disappeared. He put a wadge of cash on the table and walked out and we never saw him again. The act of acknowledging the misalignment of his fulcrum, was enough to trigger self-healing.

This example emphasizes the importance of becoming aware of these fulcrums in and around us. The treatment consisted of nothing but an awareness of the fulcrum and it had a powerful reaction from the patient.

In my view, we can have energetic fulcrums affecting us in many differing ways. They can be thoughts, feelings, sensations, or they can be physical, affecting our posture and gait. They can be nutritional, they can be the effect of illness, an accident or an operation. They can be relational - meaning these fulcrums can relate to people we are intimately related to or work colleagues. Whether they are positive or negative experiences, all of them disperse our energies in small or large ways and in various directions. Sometimes, if we are overwhelmed, our energies seem to become almost scattered to the winds.

If, though, we can start to become aware of these fulcrums, or energetic drains, which affect us in so many ways, we can bring these fulcrums together and stops our energy dispersing.

Again, as I showed in the treatment reaction described above, all we need to do is become aware of these fulcrums and something magic can happen. The fulcrums change and those little packets of energy return to us. It takes sensitivity and a degree of awareness to be able to feel these fulcrums.

Now we have some awareness of what a fulcrum is, and we are developing our sensitivity to them. The key here is not to be overly concerned with these fulcrums. Apply the basic rules again - of acceptance that they are there, allowing them to be, and observing them.

To develop our practice, we allow, accept and observe as before. In so doing we are returning our energy back into our body. Just the simple sensing and acknowledging of these fulcrums is enough, we do not have to do anything else.

If we look at our body as a field of energy, if we have energy being drawn in many directions it can literally tire us out.

So any meditative practice needs really to start with allowing all energy to return back to us. Once it has returned the practices become much, much easier.

The key is conscious awareness, this begins with the simple fact of knowing that we have fulcrums, or draws of energy away from our centre. Then by precisely acknowledging them, they return to us, restoring our energy.

Shall we try it?

Contemplation 20

Fulcrums

As I said I like to do this when I first wake up, but you can do it anytime. For this, we don't need to use the neutral or stillness of tide practices. We can use this technique to restore our energy and bring us back to neutral before doing anything else.

Start by getting a sense of yourself as a body contained within skin. Try to sense yourself as a fluid body which is slowly breathing. From this, ask your body if any of your fluid body energy is not inside you. A strange concept but don't think about it - just use this felt-sense and feel your way through this. Are you losing any energy from your body? Is it leaking out from you anywhere? Can you get a sense of your energy self?

For a moment, let's look at how our energy responds to different thoughts. Think for a second about a favourite place of yours, somewhere you love to be and that makes you happy. Just watch how your energy responds. Does some of your energy go to that place? Try to feel the movement. Now think about a loved one, and this time really picture them as if they are right there in front of you. Can you feel your energy move in front of you as if going towards that person?

Try to see if you can feel these energy pulls and try to see if you can see the fulcrum, The fulcrum can be anything, a person, a feeling, time or a sensation. It really doesn't matter.

This felt sense takes time to get, but as soon as you start to feel these pulls and fulcrums it will become very, very clear.

As soon as you feel a fulcrum or energetic pull, firstly, accept that is there. Next, allow it to be there and do not react. You may be able to feel what it is or where it comes from and you may not. It doesn't matter. What matters is that you just allow it and observe it. When you do this, a magical thing happens. The fulcrum shifts, and that piece of lost energy returns to you. It's yours and nobody else's. It could be in the form of thought, feeling sensation or something more concrete, like a dragging feeling] through your body caused by a fall or accident. Allow these sensations to be there whilst maintaining an awareness that you have a quiet, still centre.

*This is a subtle exercise that, as with everything else here, takes time to perfect. I assure you, though, that once you get the sensation, you will find it helpful, especially in situations where someone or something is draining you. Apply this practice and allow your energy to return to you. It will not have a negative effect on other people: it is **your** energy returning to you. In fact, it will help them too!*

Remember, though, that energy in the universe is limitless and, as we are an integral part of the universe, our energy is limitless too.

Chapter 21

The Fire of Ignition

In my work as an osteopath, I teach the process of ignition. It is a fascinating concept. We would say that ignition in the physiology of the body implies that there is some sort of potency in the tissues of the body. This seems to be an important prerequisite for health and the ability of the body to regulate, rebalance and heal itself.

The term *ignition* implies the act of setting something alight. It implies the use of light and fire and the process of creating some combustion with other substances.

An interesting manifestation of ignition for me is the presence of light behind the eyes. If you look at the eyes of someone who is happy, well, inspired or even in love, you tend to see a light radiating from the eyes. It is like their eyes are alight. On the contrary if you look into the eyes of someone who is tired, in grief or unwell, there is a definite absence of light. If you look at a few people, it is quite easy to see the difference. In my view this is an outer manifestation of ignition.

Put very simply, ignition implies light and light implies life. Where there is no light there is no life. Without sunlight the planet would freeze, and nothing would grow - there would literally be no life. All life needs light. Ignition implies the presence of light within. It means our internal body has connected with the presence of light.

This concept has been used in many ways. One example is when we think something new and exciting it can be described as *a light-bulb moment*. When we fall in love we can feel as if we are *basking in the light of love*. We literally shine like a light when we are in love and everybody sees it!

Another example is our journey of birth is a passage from the darkness of the womb into the light. Similarly, when dawn breaks after the darkest moments of night, it is like a slow and gentle ignition, waking up nature to the day.

In developing our Dynamics of Stillness practice, we can apply certain specific techniques to enhance this ignition. This is seemingly vital in treating someone whose immune system is low, or if they are very tired or they are in grieving.

There was a practitioner who became a student of mine a few years ago. She arrived after hours of travel to see me at the practice. She told me: "I had to visit because I have seen children treated by you and they have this wonderful light in their eyes." I told her it was not some magic but just a technique and, fortunately, I could teach it to her.

Without the light of ignition, we are not *firing on all cylinders*. This is the case whether we are in the darkness of grief and loss, or just plain tired and uninspired. Without ignition, it is hard to do even the basics of life and everything becomes a struggle, our immune systems are low, we catch everything illness going, and we can be depressed, down or unhappy.

We all need the light of ignition, which acts as a potent, aliveness within each cell in our body. It enlightens us, wakes us up to life, connects us and energizes us. Is it possible to access this ignition at will, to reconnect with the light of ignition? I think so, but it takes certain pre-requisites. It is much easier to connect with when we are well, happy and in nature. But once we learn how, we can apply this practice when we are low and down or below par health wise.

Practice 21

Ignition

The first thing we need to do here - and it is vital for this technique - is to accept exactly how we are feeling. At first, try this practice when you are feeling well and happy, but once you get the feeling of this you can try it when tired or low.

So first just allow and accept exactly how you are. Then bring your awareness to the softness in your breath. Really sense something delicate that feels sweet and soft.

At first, we can try this in nature but after a while we can do it anywhere. I will describe it in nature first.

It is a little like the technique for the Great Tide in chapter fifteen but there is an important difference.

When your nervous system becomes a little quiet, you are feeling calm and comfortable. Our thoughts start to slow down and only observe them if they arise, so they can fall away as easily as they arise.

From here, just let your sense of vision open and let it breathe out as far as the horizon. Allow it to go over the horizon and meet something that feels still.

Let your sensory awareness be open to sensing a stillness at and beyond the horizon. Wait until you get that sense of the Great Tide arising from that stillness moving slowly towards you.

Now at this point I want you to [attune to] your sensory awareness. Try to sense a quality of light within this Tide. It is there and, if you open your awareness, it can feel light.

Let this light Tide flow and pass through you. Let the lightness awaken a sense of light in every cell of your body. It feels wonderful, doesn't it? It wakes up your body's connection to the element of light. The effect is that of an ignition. It can literally light us up. Once you feel this, go look in the mirror and see how light your eyes are.

Chapter 22

Healing Breath

Breathing, as we have already found, is an important part of practice. In this chapter we will start to explore the healing potential within our breath. This is the beginning of a deeper process in our practice, which will start to look at methods of self-healing and self-care. If we start with our breath we can start to learn to rebalance our body/mind in a very gentle and supportive manner.

In many eastern practices including Hinduism, yoga, Daoism and Buddhist meditation practices, there is an emphasis on breathing. In Daoist practice, the breath is thought to be sitting at the threshold between the physical and energy bodies. Daoist philosophy looks at the movement of energy – known as *qi* (pronounced **chee**) – through specific channels called meridians running within and around the body. They feel that if the energy channels remain fluid and free without stagnation, health will be maintained. Stagnancy, in their view, causes illness. They use specific breathing techniques to help move the *qi* freely in the meridians. Yoga practice pays a lot of attention to the breath. Breathing can be calming, re-energizing and, in the case of Kriya Yoga, it is thought to be spiritually transformative.

In physical terms, breathing can say a lot about our health.

Our breathing often betrays our emotional state. If we are distressed, we often breathe fast and our breathing becomes shallow and laboured. If we are relaxed and calm, it is usually slow and steady. If we are unwell, for example if we are suffering with a fever, our breathing can be fast and irregular.

It is clear that our breathing seems to react to our state of mind and body. Maybe, if we reversed our thinking and took positive action on our breathing, we could affect the state of body mind via our breathing.

In Daoist Sung breathing the emphasis is to bring awareness to our breathing and then to direct our breath to those areas of our bodies which suffer tension and distress. This positive breathing activity is done in the hope to soften and calm the body.

As we have already mentioned, when we don't breathe effectively, our bodies suffer. Tension, whether it is physical, mental or emotional, builds up in a variety of ways. Firstly, it can tighten up our bodies and certain muscle groups, like our shoulders, our back muscles, our legs or our pelvic muscles and especially our diaphragm, the big muscle of breathing which sits as a dome shape at the bottom of our ribs. When tense and our breathing has become tight, this diaphragm muscle tightens up, which contracts our breathing further.

We must learn two new skills for this practice. The first is to learn to bring our awareness, attention and finally intention to specific parts of the body and from there to bring our awareness, attention and finally intention to our thoughts, feelings and emotions. The second follows closely on from the first. This involves bringing - via our intention - our breath, firstly to specific areas of the body and then to our thoughts, feelings and emotions.

This two-part practice sounds a little bit complex, but if we break it down it is quite easy to do. It just requires us to become aware of and able to direct our attention quite specifically.

It sounds rather an odd thing to do, to breathe into certain parts of the body, but if we use our newly developing felt-sense it is easier than you would think. The purpose of using our intention and attention to bring our breath to certain specific areas of consideration is that we are going to use our breath to change them.

For example, my lower back is sore now. I am writing, perched on a stool, not really sitting in a good posture and my lower back is getting sore. But if I start to breathe deeply, as if breathing into my lower back, I can breathe the quality of softness into my back. As I exhale, I release the accumulated tension in my lower back and it is already beginning to feel better! If this work, there is a little trick to add to make sure it works. Within any sore or blocked part of us, there is something in the block, albeit often the tiniest speck of fluidity.

It feels like a tiny sweet softness that is present within the block. If we breathe in softness to meet that tiniest softness already present within the block, something wonderful happens. That tiny speck of softness expands and grows. It can feel warm - warm, soft and fluid - as if releasing the block. So, I breathe into the block and it releases easily. Ok, it was only a minor twinge but, as with all the skills we are cultivating, the more we develop our skill-base the more powerful the response will be to the practices.

This practice is easiest to do at first if we bring awareness to specific body parts and release the accumulated tension in them. However, with practice and increased self-awareness, we can also bring this *healing breath* to feelings, thoughts and emotions. The key to this technique is to develop an increased sensitivity and awareness to how and what we are feeling.

When we start to feel areas in our body that feel not just sore but blocked or just not as full of vitality as they should be, we can start to work to release the blocks and difficult areas.

The trickier bit, of course, is applying this to our thoughts, feelings and emotions, as we often don't know how we are feeling. But we can use this time in our practice to check-in with how we are feeling with these thoughts, feelings and emotions. The clearer we can become on what our blocks are, the more we can access ways to literally breathe in softness then breathe them out and let them go.

Let's try this in a Practice, shall we?

Practice 22

Healing Breath

Let's start by sitting comfortably. It would be helpful if we can allow ourselves ten to fifteen minutes of time for this practice.

Start by checking-in as to how you are feeling. This is a good thing to get into the habit of doing. Firstly, on the physical side, just get a sense of your body, any aches, any pains or sore spots.

Let's look a little deeper now. Start with your feet. Is there anything blocked, tight or uncomfortable. Just take a note for now. Move up to your legs, pelvis, then stomach, lower back and the rest of your spine. Just take your time on this, taking note of any sore bits and potential blocks. Now focus on your chest, then your throat, neck, face, your head and then your eyes.

From this point, try to access how and what you are feeling. Are you happy, sad, feeling nothing much at all? Do you have any lingering thoughts, any feelings? Just take a note for now that they are here. The more you do this the better and more precise you can get at it.

Now hopefully you have a list of aches, spots, blocks and thoughts that you have noticed in your body.

Great now let's start to build our tools. Firstly, tune into the softness of your breath. Don't take deep breaths, just keep your breaths slightly shallow and meet something soft and sweet in your breath.

Do your usual practice of accepting and allowing anything that comes to mind in terms of thoughts, feelings and emotions, but this time let's do something different. If a thought, feeling or emotion comes up, try to fully allow yourself to feel it. As you open to the feeling of it, breathe your soft, sweet breath into that feeling. Feel it as if you are almost allowing the sweetness in the breath to penetrate the feeling of the feeling or emotion. It does not matter if the feeling is positive or negative, just breathe softness into it. As you breathe out, let it release out from you and your body. Let it out as you breathe out.

We usually have three or four layers of thoughts, feelings and emotions to work through, so we need to repeat the technique until your mind naturally gets a little quiet. You will know you have reached this point when your breathing softens more and you feel quite balanced.

Now bring your awareness to the first body area on your list. Really let your awareness and attention rest at the blocked place in your body. Now try to become more precise and detailed in your attention, in the soreness. In the block there is always a tiny bit of it that shows a little softness or fluidity. If you cannot find that tiny spot of fluidity, look more precisely. It could literally be the size of a pinhead. Once you find this little sense of fluidity in the pain or block, start to breathe in that softness to meet the fluidity in the block. As you exhale, let the block and tension release, and physically breathe it out.

Then breathe in softness and exhale tension.

Sometimes you cannot feel any fluidity in the block, especially if the pain is severe. If that's the case, try to access the idea that there could be some softness in the pain. This can work and help you to access you a little fluidity or softness within the pain. Remember to physically breathe out the tension as you exhale.

If you still cannot find any softness in the pain or block to meet with your soft breath, then spend a few minutes first by breathing softness to the block and breathing out tension. Then, after a minute or two of this, you should be able to access a little part of the pain or block that has some soft fluidity to it.

As your sweet soft breath meets the inherent softness in the block or pain, a magic thing happens. The softness in the pain increases and the pain softens and decreases. It is as if we are accessing the potential for health inside the block and, as we access this, it transforms the block.

This is a very important step in our practice as we are starting to find the underlying capacity for health in our problem areas. As we do so we start to access a deep process of self-healing. We will build on this in later chapters.

Chapter 23

Primary Breath

I have just finished a communication with a friend Tony - of course not these days a letter in the written form as we would have ten or fifteen years ago, but as a text. He talked about the importance of reconnecting with the Great Tide and its prescience right now.

The key issue we agreed on is that we are inseparable from this natural Tide or field. We also both felt that our awareness of this tide has been suppressed by schisms – separations - created by contemporary cultures and that these schisms were not present in primal cultures.

Tony (who is a sculptor) noted that 'we never disconnect from nature, but we suppress our awareness of being a holistic part of nature with our current analytical bias, blocking our ability to perceive nature as a whole'. He added that for many people it is hard to adopt or restore a holistic sensibility.

I would agree, but I would add that, for the sake of our emotional and physical health, it is important that we reconnect. It is our deep disconnection with nature that is causing us to destroy our natural environment very rapidly. In so doing, we are destroying our habitat and the future of the planet for our children and generations yet to come.

For me, the only way to combat this is through a deep and conscious reconnection with nature. I am purposefully making a reconnection with its gentle and Great Tides in and around us.

These, in turn, will reconnect us with our deepest natures and inner expression of Health, and potentially that of our communities.

In my work as an osteopath, we talk of a Primary Breath, or Primary Respiration, which breathes the body. This is an expression of the Great Tide and it is already manifest within our body. The primary breath can be felt as a gentle pulsing rhythm, which acts to breathe each cell in the body. This breathing action is like the gentle pulsing that I described in the slime mould that the biologist William Seifriz witnessed in the 1950s.

There are a variety of rhythms and rates present in the body. There is the pulse/heart rate, there is thoracic respiration which happens six to eight times a minute (at rest). There is what we call *primary respiration*. Primary respiration has two natural rates which can be felt in ourselves and nature. The first is about three to four times a minute: a gentle, breathing motion which is not confined to the lungs but can be felt everywhere in the body. It has been postulated that Primary Respiration could be the rhythm by which every cell undergoes its metabolic processes of taking in nutrients, using them to power their needs and removing waste on a cellular level. This could link with certain brainwave activity, this three to four Hertz rhythm could have some connection to delta brainwave activity and delta activity is associated with relaxation.

There is a slower rate, which corresponds to the rate of the Great or Long Tide, which is one hundred seconds for a complete cycle – fifty seconds on the inhalation and fifty seconds on the exhalation phase. This can only be felt in the body when a person goes into a deep state of relaxation. This could link to theta and other slower brainwave activity. Interestingly, when an animal is in distress this natural rhythm speeds up to eight to twelve hertz.

The funny thing is that us humans in active waking states, which are not relaxed will show this eight to twelve hertz rate which will slow as we relax to a more normal three to four hertz rate.

I am describing are normal physiological states which are not known or seen in western medicine. They can easily be felt. It takes only a small amount of time to show a person how to feel these gentle rhythmic fluid motions in the body, but it is much harder to measure.

A group of colleges spent a day at the MIT research institution in Boston USA looking at the possibility of measuring this motion. The Osteopaths taught the researchers to feel the motion, which only took ten minutes. The researchers said it would take years to devise instruments that could detect such a subtle motion whilst differentiating the more forceful motions of the lungs breathing and the heart beating.

Our human sense of touch is highly refined and can detect micro-changes in pressure whilst removing other motions. This is done by selecting exactly what we want to feel and what we want to screen out. As Osteopaths, we are trained to feel micro-changes in the environment of the body through our sense of touch. What we are looking at doing here is refining our awareness to feel this primary breathing within our own bodies first. In a later chapter, we will learn to approach other people and use our tactile awareness to feel this motion in them.

Why is it called Primary Respiration? It could be called a rhythmic motion, or a slow oscillation, but it seems to have two phases - an inhalation, which is an expansion phase and an exhalation phase, which is like a recoil phase - hence the term respiration.

It is called *primary* because it feels like it drives the fundamental processes in the body, including lung or secondary respiration. Here, for simplicity, let us call it Primary Breathing. Remember that primary breathing is like each cell in the body in harmony going through an expansion and a recoil phase.

It could be argued that this Primary Breathing is a manifestation of the way the body remains in a physiological or homeostatic harmony. Homeostasis means maintaining a steady state, which involves restoring each part of the body back to a harmonious state, a second-by-second healing or rebalancing. This is quite an amazing process, which seems to happen in a rhythmic fluid way. By tuning our awareness into this process, we are tuning our sensibility to the manifestation of Health in the body itself. It could be argued that by supporting this fluid, natural, inherent breathing process we can support the natural ability of the body towards Health.

Practice 23

Primary Breathing

Sit in a quiet comfortable position. You can adopt a standing position, or you can do this lying down. The only issue with lying down is, when you start to feel this gentle oscillation in your body, it can make you sleepy.

Get comfortable and relax your body, tune in to a degree of neutral as before with the usual allowing, accepting and observing practice and let your awareness rest on the softness of your breath.

When relaxed enough - and by now you should be finding it easy to allow your attention to move freely to parts of your body or the whole body - try to feel a degree of fluidity in the whole body. Then return your awareness to your breathing.

Once you have registered the rhythm and rate of the lung respiration, let your awareness move to your whole body. See if you can detect a slower, more profound oscillation, which is slower than that of lung breathing - about half the rate.

The motion is far more subtle but global - like every cell in your body is going through an expanding phase, and a returning phase, each cell breathing together as a whole. Can you feel this slow beautiful rhythm? If not, repeat the steps. You may only feel it in one area, but it's best if your awareness is wide, taking in your whole body, which is gently breathing in relation to nature. This is a true expression of your health and if you can maintain your awareness on this motion it is deeply calming and relaxing.

Chapter 24

Connecting Heaven and

Earth

In classical Daoism, everything in the universe is considered as an interaction between two energies, that of Yin and Yang. Yin is earth energy, the feminine, stillness, internal and quiet. Yang is creativity, activity, heaven, the male, action and change.

In the Daoist view of creation, there was an original state of oneness, called Wuji. This is known as absolute oneness. It is a point of stillness, the un-manifest Dao. It is the seed from which everything manifest comes from. It has no location and is everywhere.

From the stillness of Wuji arose two energies- that of Yang - the light expression of creation, the heavens - and Yin the denser, quieter earth energy. Yin and Yang are polar opposite energies. The ancient Daoists perceived all life in its manifest form as different interactions between these two polar energies. The intertwining energies were the qi, which as we know is a vibrational force of energy that moves everything in the universe.

The lighter, more heavenly energies of Yang the Daoists connected with our consciousness, or spirit, and psyche. Whilst the Yin energy was more of the earth, dark and dense.

It can be confusing to look at the energies of Yin and Yang as male and female energy, which is how they are often interpreted. That was not how the Daoists would look at it. They would say that man and woman each hold feminine and masculine yin and yang energies and qualities, so a woman is not Yin but a balance of Yin and Yang qualities. They referred to feminine in terms of Yin as internal, still, dark earth-like energy, with Yang being the polar opposite as creative expression, action. A person has both energies to varying degrees. The denser the energy of Yin is, of the earth, the more physical.

Man is considered the meeting point of the two polar energies of Yin and Yang. We manifest expressions of both poles to varying degrees and at varying times. From a Daoist viewpoint, our energy is constantly changing, fluctuating between these two opposites, even to tiny degrees.

The Daoists were looking to harmonize these poles to bring the practitioner closer and closer towards the state of Wuji, the un-manifest stillness before the polarity of Yin and Yang. This they considered the ultimate goal of cultivational practice.

Daoist practitioners, as I stated in the chapter on Esoteric Alchemy, practiced refining energy within the body to act to lighten the heavier earth connected Jing energy to Qi and finally to Shen, the closest to what could be considered heavenly, pure Yang energy.

The process of internal cultivation of energy was a spiritual process, which served to connect practitioners to the earthly and the celestial. And to connect these two energies.

This was part of a process of internal cultivation important to

Daoist practices.

It is an interesting and potentially transformative practice to learn to feel the Yang and Yin energies of heaven and earth and to allow them to meet and connect within our body. It is calming, energizing and enables us to feel deeply connected.

For me, the yin and yang energies both have a specific quality that can be felt within our developing sensory awareness.

The Yang energy is light and subtle, the yin is dark and rich.

There are various places in the body in which to feel this meeting of heaven and earth, but I prefer allowing the two energies to meet in my lower abdomen, a couple of inches below my umbilicus. It feels very natural there and this location was used by Daoist practitioners. They called the location Dan Tien.

I tend to do a three-stage practice for connecting Heaven and Earth. It is possible to do this practice either sitting up or lying down but I prefer to do it in a standing posture.

Practice 24

Connecting Heaven and Earth

Let's adopt a standing posture for this technique.

Ideally it is best to do this outdoors in nature, but we can do these techniques anywhere for now.

Stand with your feet shoulder width apart, hands at your sides. Now bend your knees a little and drop your pelvis - this helps to straighten your spine.

Allow your legs to relax and your spine to lengthen.

Drop your chin down a little to allow some space in the upper neck. Let your shoulders soften and relax. This should feel comfortable. N.B. If you have knee problems, try this sitting down.

*Bring your attention to the softness in your breath, using the **allow, accept and observe tools**. Bring your awareness to the softness in your breath and the fluidity within your body. Once you are feeling comfortable and neutral we can start.*

Stage 1: Heaven

Lift your palms so they are facing the sky, hands just above waist level, slightly in front of you. As you breathe in, expand your awareness up to the sky above you. Use your sensory awareness to feel a light, delicate, energy. It helps if it is sunny as the sun's energy is similar to the energy we are trying to feel in our bodies. But the energy we are trying to feel in our bodies is more than the sun. It feels like the sun and the stars and the heavens all combined. It is just as easy to feel this energy at night-time.

As you breathe in, allow this light, sun and star energy to come into your body through your head and the palms of your hand and into your lower stomach. As you breathe out, just relax and let go.

With each in-breath, feel more connection to this light energy, as if it fills your body. The main sensation will be welling in your lower stomach, but you will feel it head to toe. It is very similar to the ignition energy we felt in the chapter on Ignition.

It feels light and wonderfully peaceful.

I tend to spend four to five breaths really feeling like my body as a whole is breathing in the light energy. It is more than through my lungs. It is as if every pore is filling with light, gentle, heavenly Yang.

Once I feel a strong connection with this and a welling of warmth in my lower stomach I move onto Stage 2.

Stage 2: Earth Yin

*Keep your arms in the same position and turn the palms of your hands this time to face **downwards** towards the earth. I like to* *get a sense of the earth and its energy first. It is not light, like the heavenly energy, but it is delicate and strong and equally peaceful, with a deeper quality of feeling.*

Expand your awareness firstly to a point about thirty centimetres below your feet. Really feel the connection to the earth.

As you breathe in, allow the Yin energy of the earth to rise up through the mid-sole of your feet and into your lower stomach again. As you breathe out, let go and let the energy move back down through the soles of your feet into the earth. This is a wonderfully grounding, energizing feeling. It can be especially helpful in releasing tension if you can let go to the earth with each outbreath.

Continue this stage until you feel energized, connected and you have released all your tensions.

Stage 3: Combining Heaven and Earth

For this final stage, we are going to bring our hands to a more neutral position facing the front of your lower stomach. Keep your fingers relaxed and comfortable. Keep your arms raised slightly. Now imagine a large ball in your hands and hold them as if to hold that ball just in front of you.

At this point, we are going to split our attention in two directions as we combine the last two techniques together. On your in-breath, breathe in from above and below - both heaven and earth - at the same time drawing in both energies until both energies meet beautifully and delicately in front of your lower stomach.

The feeling is energizing and peaceful. The two different

165

qualities meet in your lower stomach and blend into a delicate energy that holds both elements. This can be hard to feel at the beginning but, as with all these techniques, it gets easier each time we do it.

My usual morning practice starts with running and stretching, followed by this standing practice, which I find personally invaluable for its ability to rebalance, reconnect and energize me. It leads naturally onto connecting with the Great Tide and other processes. After that I go directly into a sitting posture for some meditation work.

Chapter 25

Dynamic Stillness

This book is called "Dynamics of Stillness'. When you think about it does that make sense? Stillness is defined of as a lack of motion. So how does that make sense?

How can you have a dynamic within Stillness?

This is what we will explore in this chapter.

In the last chapter, we looked at the Daoist concept of Wuji, the un-manifest Dao, or unified energy from which arises the manifest, or creation and form. But, by its nature, Wuji has the potential from which all motion manifests.

In our practice so far, when we have started to experience Stillness - for example, in the Practices on The Stillness Around Us and the one on Stillpoints - the stillpoint or stillness we feel is imbued with a sense of potency, like a potential energy. As we start to develop our relationship with the stillness around and inside us, we will start to sense differing qualities within it.

When teaching palpation and sensory awareness to my colleagues, there is a quality, which we call Dynamic Stillness, which can be felt when we feel the Long/Great Tide and how its slow breathing motion is affecting the tissues of the patient. If we open our awareness further and meet the stillness from which the tide arises, it is like we move through a doorway into another sense. This is a very light, almost translucent quality of stillness, which has a quiet but great power.

This Dynamic Stillness has a fascinating quality. It feels continuous, meaning it feels like the body of the patient dissolves into it, becoming translucent without form. When we are treating a patient and we wait with this light quality of Dynamic Stillness, an interesting thing happens. It feels like the body of the patient starts to reform, like it is recreating itself. It feels wonderfully peaceful for both the patient and practitioner. This sensory experience is quite common when treating patients. It can be induced with the steps above or it can happen spontaneously.

Of course, the patient does not dissolve into light, but they can feel certain phenomena happening to themselves. When I first had this treatment applied to me, it felt like I was floating just a couple of inches above the table, like I was levitating. I wasn't, of course, but it felt rather free and very peaceful!

My understanding of Dynamic Stillness has been acquired through years of feeling it, especially when I have been working on patients. I have also felt it when I have been doing sitting practices of meditation.

When this quality of Dynamic Stillness appears, it feels like the boundary between me and the universe dissolves and I am totally part of a perfect oneness with the universe. This is dynamic stillness. The feelings of peace, connection and oneness are difficult to describe without feeling them. It is wonderful!

I think this quality must be like the Wuji in Daoism.

I don't think it takes twenty years of meditating in a cave or monastery to develop the ability to experience Dynamic

Stillness. However, some clear building steps are needed. These focus on developing our connection to stillness, alongside developing sensory awareness, connecting with nature and learning to allow and accept [what we are experiencing]. The final step is observing our own thoughts, feelings and emotions. This means we learn to start accepting ourselves a little, which in turn can bring humility.

If we practice this work with an ego, or a sense of owning it, we will not get very far. We will just go around in circles. This work is not anything we can own. If we are lucky, we can catch a glimpse of the sheer wonder of life and its interconnectedness. Experiencing this is truly breathtaking.

The practices require a developing humility and a deepening connection to nature and to each other. This brings with it a respect for all life and maybe a wish to protect and preserve all life.

What is interesting is that this practice starts to change us. As we connect deeply to ourselves, nature, each other and the universe, our sense of responsibility changes. If we are all interconnected, we must care for and nurture one another. This is the most beautiful and natural thing in the universe. If we all learn to feel it and connect with it, surely, we would develop a deeper responsibility to the planet and each other.

The unusual feeling that we start to sense our body edges dissolving - becoming transparent, so there is no boundary between us and the surrounding Stillness - this feeling is new and wonderful.

Practice 25

Dynamic Stillness

For this practice we are going to try two very different methods to gain some sensory awareness and experience of Dynamic Stillness

Sitting with Heaven and Earth

For this practice we are going to build on our last technique of connecting heaven and earth. This time we will adopt a sitting posture. Sit comfortably in whatever posture suits and feels comfortable.

The lotus positions, especially the full lotus, were thought to be preferred in Hindu and Buddhist teachings. In this posture, the palms and soles of the feet are facing the sky. I am still not flexible enough to do the Lotus, so I sit with a cushion under my bottom. The extra height makes it easier to cross my legs.

When you are comfortable in your chosen position, place your hands in your lap, palms facing upwards.

Tune into the softness of your breath and allow your body to come to neutral. This process should be quite easy by now. You have probably already noticed that] the more you do, it the easier it gets.

Now we are going to repeat what we did with the Connecting Heaven and Earth technique. To recap, as you breathe in, become aware of a light delicate energy from above. The quality is like sunlight but slightly more. It is like the subtle energy of the sun, stars and planets, or the universe as a whole. Breathe this energy into your lower stomach through every pore in your body, especially the top of your head and the palms of your hands.

As you repeat this five or six times, you should feel this soft light energy fill you and deeply calm you. When you feel this quality fill you, especially your lower stomach, we are now [ready] to engage with the earth energy.

Turn your palms face down and start by feeling a slightly stronger, deeper vibrant quality of the earth. Widen your awareness to the earth around you and see if you can feel this quiet, deeply nurturing energy.

As you breathe in, let the energy come into every pore, especially via your palms and the soles of your feet and into your lower stomach. Repeat this for five to six breaths so you really get the sense of this nurturing earth energy in your body.

Now just rest your hands again on your lap in a neutral position. From here, you want to try to combine the above techniques. Split your awareness. On each in-breath, breathe in both heaven and earth energies from above and below. Breathing out relax. Repeat this five or six times, relaxing more with each outbreath.

You may start to get a sense of developing Stillness within the motion of breathing. It should begin to feel like both energies you are breathing start to become one. Let this quality develop and the deep stillness - a dynamic stillness - develop. You may get a sense that you are becoming light and full of this energy. This energy is the same inside and outside you, all around you and to the horizon. It is a deep and dynamic stillness that feels perfect, connected and deeply peaceful.

After a few minutes this sensation will naturally come to an end and you will start to feel a gentle fluidity, an inherent natural motion in your body and your awareness of your surroundings will return. This is a natural end to the process.

The Stillness in the Tide

You may wish to try this technique immediately after the last one or you may find you want to come back to this one next time you practice. If you get a nice experience of Dynamic Stillness, that is often enough.

For this practice, we are going to build on our technique for feeling the Great Tide, which we looked at in chapter 15.

It is best to be sitting with a view of a horizon. As we get used to these techniques, though, you will find that you will have less need to [have visual] access to landmarks and processes.

Let us try this technique with our eyes closed this time.

Sit comfortably and quietly with your eyes closed and allow your awareness to go slowly out, as if breathing it out to the horizon. You don't need a direction, rather you need an overall awareness of a horizon. This time, instead of seeing it, feel it with your developing felt sense. Let your awareness just breathe out to the horizon and let it meet the stillness that is already at the horizon. Can you feel it?

Once you have accessed this Stillness, just wait with it and enjoy that feeling. After a little while, you will feel the Tide slowly arising from the Stillness on the horizon and slowly come towards you from one side. It isn't important where it comes from as this is a perceptual quality. Sometimes, it can approach from all sides. Let it breathe you, in other words, let it breathe through you, passing undiminished. The feeling is that you become connected to, or even become part of, this Great Tide.

Next, we are going to develop this a little more. As you feel the gentle movement of the Tide, I want you to find somewhere in it - it could be the horizon, or it could be a sensory quality within the motion - that is Stillness. It is the Stillness that is behind the Tide.

As you access this fulcrum, something shifts in your perception. You start to feel a quality of Dynamic Stillness. This quality has total stillness, but it also has a great power in it, like a potential energy from which motion manifests. It is more than motion, everything manifests from this Dynamic Stillness.

You can start to get a sense that you are a translucent, transparent part of this Dynamic Stillness. It is quiet yet powerful and it has an almost sacred quality to it.

Enjoy this quality for a little while - a few seconds to a few minutes - and be aware of the end point of it. It is very interesting. It feels like you are reforming, almost like an egg reforming. The quality is one of wholeness, like you are being re-created in that moment.

Chapter 26
Returning to the Natural - True Creativity

One of our many purposes in this work is to start to return to a natural response to life, moved by the moment and to start to lose our conditioned responses to everyone and everything around us. In Daoism this has been termed 'the seat of spontaneity'.

True spontaneity has great potential for ourselves. By its nature it is deeply creative - meaning we start to create our lives moment by moment. This state of being is almost childlike. We start to release historic, conditioned responses to life and start to act as opposed to react to life and its great ups and downs.

This process starts with the simple step of learning to find a neutral state within ourselves. It proliferates as we develop a deepening connection and understanding of Stillness within and around us. We learn to feel the great natural Tides in nature and learn to experience Dynamic Stillness. Dynamic Stillness creates the potential from which life creates itself moment to moment as motion from stillness and, as we experience and learn these things, it can slowly change us.

At the same time, we are looking at our senses and how they have been conditioned by our life experiences. We will develop this in the next chapters. We will learn to release the conditioning of our senses in the hope of starting to experience life and the universe anew.

As our rhythm connects and slows to the natural rhythms in nature, this can progress. We start to feel our way through life, which brings a natural creativity and spontaneity.

True Creativity

What does it mean to be truly creative? Creative people tend to think for themselves, often tasked with thinking ahead of the group. In indigenous tribes, like the Bushmen of the Kalahari, the artists would paint beautiful cave paintings. They were tasked within the tribe to scribe, describe, document and inspire the tribes.

I am a great fan of art. Since they were a young age, my children have been dragged to galleries around the world and introduced to many great artworks.

For me, the true artists inspired their own cultures, and sat at the cutting edge in the development of cultures. The great artists lead the way for the people in defining and understanding man and his relationship to nature and the divine. This process may have been lost to some degree in recent generations but in principle the artist, the sculptor, the writer and the architect would be at the spearhead in the development of culture.

The true artist has pure spontaneous creativity. They engage with their surroundings and interpret them in ever new ways, spontaneously moved to act in response to their senses.

But I feel that every one of us can be the artist of our lives - no matter what we are doing. If we act spontaneously and creatively in response to our senses, we are being totally creative in each moment and our life can become an art-form, a work of ever-changing art. It doesn't matter if we are painting pictures, painting the walls, caring for a baby or doing the washing up - it really is not important. Once we are in rhythm with life and come from a true place of spontaneity we become truly creative.

The process of 'returning to the natural' means we learn to consciously let go of conditioned responses to life. We become neutral to ourselves and, in doing so, we start to practice self-awareness and, most importantly, self-acceptance. With increased self-acceptance, something magical happens. As we allow, accept and observe and finally become neutral to ourselves, we judge ourselves less and less. In doing so, we start to judge others less and less and learn to accept others. This brings with it a deeper sense of compassion and empathy.

Coming from 'the natural' includes greater self- acceptance, and in that greater acceptance for others there is a growing sense of neutral and connection to Stillness, and Dynamic Stillness. With it there is a deepening connection to nature and the Tide, bringing a spontaneity and true creativity within each moment.

The unusual experience of feeling like your body dissolves into Stillness, becoming transparent - when you enter a state of Dynamic Stillness - can act to make us more transparent. In that state, we are less affected by and having less effect on the nature around us. It is almost like we become able to step with a lighter footprint.

Practice 26

The Seat of Spontaneity

For this practice, we use the building blocks we have been using in each chapter:

We find a quiet place to sit for a while. We enter a state of Neutral by allowing accepting and observing thoughts, feelings and emotions - we just let it all be.

From here, we meet a deepening sense of stillness that is ever present around us. Let that outside presence of Stillness penetrate. As our minds settle and calm, our presence increases.

From here, let your awareness breathe out to the horizon - this time, eyes closed so we can use our felt-sense to feel the stillness on the horizon. From here, wait for the Tide to come in, to move from Stillness to action as it breathes us.

When you can get a solid sense of the Tide, follow it returning to the horizon and go again to the fulcrum of Stillness from which it comes. This can bring a sense of a deeper Stillness with a power. You can sense a softening of your own body's 'edges" and a quality of Dynamic Stillness, power and potential within Stillness.

From here, bring your attention and awareness back to yourself. See yourself, connected to the Tide and through it to the underlying Dynamic Stillness within the universe or multiverse.

Wait at this fulcrum point from which the Dynamic Stillness is pregnant with expression, wanting to create the manifest from the un-manifest. From here, allow yourself to be moved by the Dynamic Stillness of the universe to create. Try to feel out how the Universe is creating this moment for you and what you need to do right now. Try to use this Dynamic within the stillness to guide a deep instinctual part of yourself.

Again, this process is all about developing a deeper sense of connection to this deep, instinctual part of ourselves, where we are not driven by history or ego, but we are alive and responsive to the Universe in the moment.

Allow yourself to be moved by the moment freely and fluidly. It feels wonderful doesn't it? Trust it and trust yourself. It feels like you are being held by life, safe and aware. It is like sitting in the seat of spontaneity, totally free to be moved by the moment.

Chapter 27

Stillness Proliferates

As our practice develops and deepens, there are a number of positive processes that occur. These are not controlled by our technique - they start to occur spontaneously. It is like planting seeds in well-tended, watered soil with the right sunlight and weather conditions, which in our practices we are starting to create. But what is growing in us is more than the practice. It is the beautiful flower that we planted as a seed, or the wonderful fruit that we never expected would grow. The fruits here are numerous.

Firstly, I hope we start to become more accepting and more neutral to ourselves, which means we give ourselves a break, practicing more self-love and self-care. An interesting side-effect of greater self-love is that we naturally become more accepting of others, i.e. we give everyone else a break too!

Through the practices, we also develop a deepening relationship to the Great Natural Stillness that is all around us always. We tune our senses to it so can feel it at will and it can start to enter our consciousness spontaneously as Stillpoints, or times of Stillness.

We also deepen our relationship to our internal stillness, to still-points and an underlying stillness that is always there. This starts to enter our everyday life and people around you can start to enjoy an increased feeling of peace when they are around you.

By connecting with the Tide, our natural rhythms slow down. Feeling calm, we start to feel a deeper connection with nature.

By aligning ourselves to Dynamic Stillness we can start to feel truly spontaneous, moved by the moment, and almost as if we are aligned to the Universe.

Through all these combined processes our practice naturally deepens. We must think less and less about how to practice and we can now spend more time in deep, quiet states.

One side effect of this is that we start to lose our sense of time when practicing. We think we have been sitting, enjoying Dynamic Stillness for five to ten minutes but when we look at the clock it's been more like forty to fifty minutes.

There is a natural proliferation of Stillness that occurs. It is like our body/mind starts to completely relax into the Stillness which, as we sit, slowly takes shape, proliferates and deepens. It also has a bigger feeling of power, or Dynamic, quality to it. It is like a gentle, growing process that happens between ourselves and the Universal Stillness. It is a relationship that grows, or a flower or tree that, once the right conditions exist, grows spontaneously.

What is important here, in my view, is to be aware of this natural growing, proliferation, deepening Stillness which grows that little bit each time (with natural peaks and troughs depending on our mood). If we bring our awareness to the process of proliferation, it grows even more.

Practice 27

Stillness Proliferates

For this practice we start in the same manner we always do, but once you start to feel Stillness, either in or around you, or the Tide or Dynamic Stillness, just stop doing anything. Just sit, relax and watch as Stillness naturally proliferates. We are not bringing our awareness to anything: we are sitting, allowing our awareness to be breathed by the moment, with no technique just enjoying this deepening process.

Try to sense this naturally spontaneous proliferating Stillness and how it develops. Ask yourself - what is deepening it?

Chapter 28

Meeting Our Health

As we start to feel a deepening connection to natural rhythms outside in nature and inside our body and as we deepen our relationship to Stillness and Dynamic Stillness, a natural progression is to start to orientate ourselves to our capacity for Health.

The World Health Organization defines Health as a level of functional and metabolic efficiency of a living organism. They go on to say that Health is 'a state of complete physical, mental, and social wellbeing and not merely the absence of disease and infirmity.'

This definition has prevailed since 1948, though it is seen as controversial mainly due to its abstract nature.

Following a three-year global study, a researcher named Alex Jadad came up with another definition of health: 'Health is conceptualized as the ability to adapt and self-manage when individuals and communities face physical, mental or social challenges.'

What I like about the second definition is that this acknowledges that we are not isolated beings. As such, we function within layers of interrelating fields, communities and connections, all of which have a degree of interdependency between the individual and the group.

What we are interested in for our practice is to explore our own relationship to Health. What does Health mean for you? A healthy body, a healthy mind, to love and be loved? A healthy relationship with ourselves and others, with our community? With our children? Our parents? With our lover? Can I be healthy if my body is not quite right?

Health for me is a perception. It is a perception of self which develops very early on in our lives. It relates to the idea of consciousness and, by consciousness, I mean self-awareness. Consciousness is defined as *an awareness of one's own existence, sensations, thoughts, feelings, individually or collectively*. If we look at consciousness more deeply, we could break it down further into:

1) Proprioception, meaning our ability to sense our body in space. This is mostly governed by proprioceptor receptors in and around our joints

2) Exteroception, meaning our outer senses, our touch, smell, hearing, vision and taste

3) Interoception, meaning our perception of our internal world made up from receptors in our skin and internal organs, like hunger receptors, pain receptors in our skin, and proprioceptors in our organs, for example, the pancreas.

These senses are then filtered through the higher centres of our brain, combining with our emotional state and our thoughts and beliefs. The result of all this activity combines to give us a sense of consciousness - awareness of our *self* and of our surroundings.

There is one more sense, which we have mentioned: the *felt-sense*, which uses a combination of our senses and proprioceptive awareness to sense Stillness, Tides and Fluidity. As we work to become neutral, we are trying to unlock this 'felt-sense' from our thoughts, beliefs, emotions and feelings.

An important part of this journey for me is to start to learn to feel our Health. Health is more than a concept: it is something that can be felt within our body. What is more, if we can learn to tune in to this Health, we can learn to harness it to heal ourselves and, eventually, to heal other people.

Health has a sensory quality, a felt-sense that feels like a gentle, fluid, light expression - a motion - that is present within the body. There is an inherent freedom in the expression a motion or a freedom to move. This can be felt in a specific local area or in the whole body. To feel it, we need certain prerequisites. We have learned these prerequisites on this journey into our practice.

Let's just look again at how our senses, both interior and exterior, are patterned from very early on, before we are born. My feeling is that we orientate early on in our lives to the opposite of Health. By this I mean that we become attuned to what *hurts*, what *feels blocked* and what *doesn't* feel nice.

There is an important reason for this orientation to pain and blockage: self-preservation.

Our pain receptors mainly in the skin, less in organs, start their life early. By about 30 weeks *in utero*, the foetus has developed these nocireceptors, which are present throughout the body in the dermal skin layers. The response to pain in a foetus is diffuse as the higher brain centres haven't 'wired up' yet. A full-term baby has most of its pain receptors present, but there are fewer present on the top and the back of the head. This is so that the incredible pressure of birth doesn't cause pain - and then distress - to the baby. But soon after birth the sensory centres of the brain wire up.

Pain is an interesting phenomenon. What is pain? Is it prostaglandins near an injury site being released, stimulating nerve endings and transmitting back via the spinal cord, then up to the thalamus in the mid-brain, where pain is first felt and then back to sensory cortex, where the pain becomes conscious.

According to Pattern Theory of Pain, nerve impulses combine to telegraph Morse Code like messages to the spinal cord and brain. Some pains are reflex to the spinal cord – like flinching if we touch a hot stove. A prick of the skin may not hurt most, but it hurts the fastest, moving at 98ms. Burning or aching pain travels slower [through the body].

Pain is not a fixed perception. This means that we can alter our response to pain. There are gates at various levels of the brain, which allow input from cognitive/emotional or other senses. This can alter the sensation of pain and make it either more or less painful. For example, you can elicit a soothing response by putting a baby to a mother's breast after a painful injection. This acts to modify the response of the body to pain.

This is just an example using pain sensors. All our senses, whether they are internal or external, are open to be modulated by our feelings, thoughts, emotions and beliefs. [Pain] acts to rewire our brains.

What is important to bring from this is that our experience of Health is complex. It comes from sensory experience and emotional makeup, both of which was wired into our brains early on. What is more important than that in my view is that our thoughts, feelings and perceptions of our Health can be remodelled and reshaped into something that is better for us.

We need our internal and external sensory awareness to ascertain if there is danger in our environment. For example, we move our hand away from a hot stove. Or, in our [primitive] history, we learned to fight or run from a wild animal.

This focus on 'problems' has focused away from gaining a good relationship with what actually feels nice, well, and healthy in our body.

We do know how to feel this. Our nervous systems have a deep memory of the comfort of a mother's touch, of her smell, [of soothing] sound. Our senses can be soothed by beauty, by wonderful tasting foods and by human touch. But rarely are we focused on that abstract sense of health, of feeling the potential for wellbeing within our body. This is compounded by the overwhelming external noise, the media, the pace of life and by our constant sensory overload.

Where is there time and space to feel this delicate expression of Health in our body? But it is vital [that we find the time to do so]. There is an old adage which says, 'what you focus on grows'. I think this is true.

As I write this chapter, I am snowed in at my practice in Ireland. I am meant to be in London today, but I am here. It is so amazingly beautiful. I have a warm space, candles are lit and there is a gentle picture of snow falling. It is creating a winter wonderland and a perfect retreat! But last night, I mistakenly switched on the TV, and spent the next two hours watching media tales of woe. I found myself panicking and feeling I would be stuck here forever. I became distressed.

I had started to do something that we all do sometimes. I focused on the negative. What struck me was how quickly I became anxious. I rarely watch TV, but I slipped into it. It took some practice/meditation and going out to feed the birds to restore my inner calm.

We have learnt since we were very young to focus on what feels 'wrong' in our bodies. To learn to self-heal, we must re-pattern our brain to not feeling what is *wrong*, but what feels *right*, what feels Healthy, fluid and even light in the body.

I spend much time teaching palpation and perceptual studies to Osteopaths. In the Daisy Clinic, we treat children with complex special needs, often with a variety of difficult issues to overcome. The first thing I teach the Osteopaths is to refocus their feeling sense away from what feels blocked.

In truth, many of these children have such blocks within their body if we focus on them it just acts to tire the child and the practitioner. But if we focus on something that is free - some delicate fluid expression, somewhere in their body - and follow that, the treatment can start to be effective. How simple is that as a philosophy? But it is difficult for the students to begin with. Their entire education was focused on finding the lesion and not the Health, so it can be a real challenge to begin with.

To refocus on the Health and to learn to self-heal we must go through a series of steps. Can you guess what they are? Yes - they are what we have been building each chapter until now. We have been starting with developing a practice. We are trying to re-pattern our brains here. Re-patterning our brains is literally rewiring them. Like creating a new path to walk on it takes repeated work, practice to create the new path.

Next, we need those three tenets of Acceptance, Allowing and Observing our thoughts, feelings, emotions and even our beliefs. We need to deepen our relationship to Stillness, Dynamic Stillness and the Tide. From here we can start to re-orientate our senses, internal, external and Felt-sense to the Health.

Let's try that now.

Practice 28

Meeting the Health

Let's settle comfortably and sit. This time, just bring your attention and awareness to the Stillness around you. Wait for that Stillness to calm you to neutral. By now, your body is repatterning and knowing the path and deepening its connection to Stillness.

Now bring your awareness to a patch of skin on your hand if your hands are facing down. Sense the weight of the air on your skin. Can you feel it?

This is bringing your sensory awareness specifically to one spot and sensing something that we tune out - we tune out most sensory impressions or there would be too many!

Now bring your awareness to your skin. Can you feel the air on it all? It doesn't matter if you feel it through your clothes, you can still feel it.

Now just for fun, place one hand on the other and apply a little pressure. Try to really feel it as it pushes down on your pressure receptors in your skin.

Next, I want you to shift your awareness to the inside of your body. How does it feel? Can you put a name on it, are you tired? What does tired feel like? What is its quality? Can you feel something uncomfortable in your body? How does that feel? Can you name it?

Now let's switch our perception. Is there anywhere in your body that feels nice, feels fluid, delicate, light, feels free to move? Allow your awareness to meet any location in your body that feels nice and let your attention rest there. What happens? Does that fluid feeling expand?

Now bring your awareness to your skin again. Feel the weight of the air on it. Now soften your awareness, allow your skin, your edges to soften, to become more fluid and breathe. It usually starts in one place, then other areas catch up until everything just feels soft and fluid around your edges.

Just enjoy that quality for a few minutes and then bring your awareness to what is around you and sense when you feel the Tide coming.

Chapter 29

Self-Healing

Is it possible to heal oneself? Can we have any influence at all on the balance and healthiness of our body? We often have the perception that our body systems 'do their thing' without our interference. But we do have an influence always on the potential for health within our body. Everything we ingest can be harmful or helpful to our body. Each food [choice we make] can be good or bad for us, and often a little of both.

Toxicity in our environments can have a large effect on our health and wellbeing. Even our emotions have been shown now to influence our body. Often, stress - or distress - has been shown to agitate certain elements of our nervous systems and have a knock-on effect on our immune systems.

Our health then seems to be a complex combination of the natural balance within our body, and its response to the environment we inhabit - emotional, nutritional, other potential toxic elements or our genetic tendencies.

In the last chapter, we looked at our own perception of health. We looked in detail at a possible way we put together our perception of our health.

But how closely connected are our perception of health and our actual health. In [my osteopathy?] practice I meet very healthy people whose perception of their health is poor, for whatever beliefs they hold, and their emotional state have strong effects on health perception.

In the opposite way I often meet people who are quite unwell, with cancer or chronic disease states, but who have positive perceptions of their health. They often seem more attuned to the potential for their health than the underlying disease state.

We see that health, to a large degree, comes down to our perception of it. I would argue that the first step in the process of self-healing is to alter our perception of health – to change our underlying view of how we perceive our body, from one of looking at the problems, the lesions, to looking at the potential health that is always there, even if we are quite ill.

I outlined in the last chapter that this is the first stage, but how can we move on from this to attempt to start to heal ourselves? Is it even possible to influence our internal physiology? I would argue that we could change these internal states to varying degrees, depending on the underlying potential for health. If we learn to focus on and pay attention to the inner natural healing processes within our body, the act of paying attention to them increases their potency and effect.

The act of focusing is a basic principal of treating a patient with osteopathy. We treat patients with a wide variety of issues by learning to find the potential for health within the body and supporting that internal process. If this is applied very precisely, this simple idea can be profound.

Each of us has an incredible potential to heal and restore function in areas that are not functioning properly. We do so every second of our lives. It is called *homeostasis*, meaning [the process of] maintaining an internal steady state, or a state of physiological balance. This happens constantly within our bodies, from the simplest to the most complex ways. For example, our body metabolizes its food needs, [and so] creating energy and waste products, which [in turn] are processed by the body. If we train hard and strain a muscle group, very quickly it heals itself unless the strain is too much. If we break a bone, it usually heals in days to weeks. The body is incredible at this [process of healing itself].

Disease often occurs if these self-healing mechanisms fail us, if the strain is too much, if the break is too bad or, if the natural chemistry of the body stops functioning correctly, a state of dis-ease ensues. But can we [directly] affect this? Can we enhance our body's ability to heal? I would argue that we can. [I would also argue that] we can heal others. I will introduce the process of healing others in coming chapters.

[In order to properly self-heal] We need to set up certain preconditions for the techniques of self -healing to be effective. If we don't do this, [self-healing] become very hard to achieve. But as with all these practices, practice makes perfect! To do this, we become neutral to ourselves and learn to allow our attention to gently stay with these tiny, delicate forces as they act within our body - these fluid, light potencies acting to restore function and balance. The trick here is that what we focus on grows, so by giving precise attention to these forces, a magic thing seems to happen. These forces grow, which gives a wonderful warm, healing sense to the tissue we are focusing on. If we repeat this a few times, the body can start to engage with it quite easily, and with these growing expressions, the hope is that they can help the body try to find a better expression of health or balance.

I would argue that if we focus our awareness correctly, this technique can be helpful when conditions are severe. This technique for me can be equally helpful in dealing with acute and chronic pain, even if it is severe. But with severe pain, like bone pain from secondary cancer or the severe neurological pain suffered in Trigeminal neuralgia, it takes a massive effort of will [power] [for the sufferer] not to be[come] overwhelmed with the pain.

I have taught these techniques to people with both these conditions, which are some of the worst pains imaginable. In both situations, these patients have reported some lessening of pain. But whatever the situation, from severe metastatic pain to feeling a little under the weather or a minor ache in your little finger, to just the idea of supporting your body's health, the technique remains the same.

We can apply the same practice to emotional states too. If we are feeling weighed down by grief, sadness or depression, we can apply the following technique to soften the feelings and make them more manageable.

Practice 29

Self-Healing

For this practice, we need all the skills we have learned so far, along with the appliance of undivided attention for a certain time period.

Start by sitting comfortably or lying down comfortably. This will take a little time the first time you try it and, as with everything we do here, it gets easier each time we practice it.

Tune in to something that feels soft, fluid and delicate within your breathing. From here, allow and accept all the thoughts, feelings and emotions that arise. Observe them rising and falling away for a few minutes.

Next bring your awareness to the Stillness that is all around us and try to sense a quality of Stillness within your body.

Now, start to bring your awareness to a sense of some part of you that feels fluid and healthful, even light in its quality. It could be the tiniest micro spot of fluidity somewhere but, if you wait, something will show up. Allow this sense of fluidity to breathe, to expand naturally - just by bringing your awareness to it.

Wait with this part of the practice for a few minutes until you start to get a sense of fluidity in your whole body, almost like it becomes one drop of water. If this doesn't happen, don't worry, just keep your awareness on something that feels sweet and fluid.

Now change your attention to feel somewhere in your body that feels blocked, dark and non-fluid. Just focus on it lightly. Do not go into it too much.

Now [focus on] that small bit of your awareness on the blocked bit - that light awareness. Within the block there is the tiniest speck of light and fluidity. Sometimes it just feels like the memory of light, fluid potency, just a tiny spot of it within the block. It is always there. Sometimes, you must wait, with the knowledge and trust that it is there. When you see that fluidity, completely focus your attention on it. Forget the rest of the block and keep your attention on the light, fluid potential.

Something amazing happens here. The light fluid bit starts to grow, and in doing so, it starts to change the surrounding block, softening and lightening it. Keep your awareness on the light fluid speck as it grows. It starts to meet the general fluidity in the body.

As the block softens and lightens, the fluids in the body start to get quiet and still. Often, the body enters a still point. At this point, open your awareness to the stillness all around you and you may feel the Tide come in.

The end point is when everything returns to a gentle fluidity. The block may not have gone completely, but it will feel somewhat better.

The principle is the same with pain and with difficult emotions. Just go through the same steps and stay with the potential for lightness and fluidity, even within the darkest feeling. Sometimes you just must trust in the potential for the lightness to come, even if you cannot see it at first. If you get stuck just go back to allowing whatever [wants to come to] come, accepting then observing, and bringing your attention back to the potential for an expression of health. [This expression] is always there, it is just hidden sometimes, especially if the pain is severe.

At the beginning, try this once or twice. As you get good at it, it starts to get easier and something almost more important starts to happen which is that you start to change your focus onto your health, [rather than on any pain]. [The effect of this] can be profound.

Chapter 30

Meeting the Health

in Others

In the last two chapters we started to change our way of looking at ourselves. We have moved away from seeing our own blocks, deficits and lesions, whether they are physical, emotional or spiritual. From there, we went on to try to feel what Health felt like in ourselves. The practice then developed from there into attempting a process of self– healing.

These principles are important to gain an experience of and a developing relationship to before we go on to applying them to others.

Others in this case are friends, family other people but also fauna and flora- nature itself. We can learn to apply these principles to treating pets, or even suffering plants. There will be more of that in the next chapter.

What we must start with is, once again, a fundamental change in perspective, followed by a developing sensory experience of what Health feels like in another person. To meet the Health in others, we must first be open to the idea of it. Just as with our view of ourselves, we are usually all too aware of the faults in others, even our loved ones. We can focus our attention on what irritates us about those around us, interspersed with feelings of love. For this practice, we must become conscious of our own thinking about others and make the necessary changes to it. What I am saying here is that, for these purposes, we must actively choose to see something quite lovely, perfect and beautiful about another person or living thing, [who or whatever] we are choosing to focus on. I am not saying that we ignore [difficult] issues in the other, but [rather that we] bring our attention directly onto something that is sweet, delicate and fluid in the other. This is before we even touch them. The sense comes first from our mental viewpoint.

It is an interesting exercise to do. We will play with this idea in the Practice exercise. If we can meet the health of another person, see something nice first in a loved one, it should be easy.

If we try to see something quite lovely - even just the tiniest idea of something that is sweet, or even likable about someone or something that we find repugnant - that is much harder. But it is quite freeing to do, even [if we can only do it] for the tiniest second.

If we are going to try to engage a healing process in another [person], we must first start with this [different, more positive way of] thinking. it is absolutely vital.

This practice brings to my mind a Tibetan Buddhist practice called 'Loving Kindness'. In it one chants or says to oneself the following:

May I be happy, may I be well.

Then after repeating this a few times you bring your attention to another person. You first think of a loved one and say:

*May **you** be happy, may **you** be well.*

From here you bring your attention to someone who you know but don't either like or dislike. You feel neither way, say the bank teller or someone you see on the bus.

*May **they** be happy, may **they** be well.*

Now you can bring your attention to someone you really dislike. They may have harmed you or others and are repugnant to you:

*May **they** be happy, may **they** be well.*

The clever part of this practice is that it refocuses our attention on the Health in others and ourselves. On a subtler level, it works to bring a level of self-acceptance to elements within ourselves that are repugnant to us, to the bit of us that we are not happy with.

If the outer world is just a reflection of our interior world - accepting and wishing well to others who you do not like - it must reflect a level of self-love. This is a [very] healing practice and one you should spend a few minutes a day trying. There is something in the practice that is liberating and beautiful.

For our purposes, then, we must first select the person or thing we wish to engage with. This is much easier to do with something or someone we love because it is easy to meet their Health. We can graduate to healing others who we are not moved to naturally love later! It doesn't matter what element of this person you focus on. You could turn your attention just to their hair, or to their outfit, or to the way they smile, or the sweet love they show. Just focus on one element of the person that is sweet and allow yourself to really get a feeling of your love of that element.

What I am asking here is to feel what it feels like in you to like something about another. Ok let's try this [in our Practice].

Practice 30

Meeting the Health in Others

For this first part of the practice of Healing another, we do not need anyone else there. We can use our feelings and our imagination - that is enough for our purposes now.

Choose firstly someone you love. Close your eyes and try to 'feel' what it feels like to love them. Is it a warm glow in your chest, or is it a quiet, gentle, sweet feeling? Or is it an overwhelmingly strong feeling. It doesn't matter what the feeling is, just allow yourself to feel it.

From here bring your attention to something that you adore about this person. Is it their smile, the way they talk to you, their generosity or their inner beauty? Whatever it is, allow yourself to feel how that makes you feel.

Remember that feeling – we are going to come back to it later.

Now let's try doing the same for someone you barely know: the shop assistant, the man on the bus, the someone you feel neither positive nor negative towards. It helps if you can remember them a little. Now focus your awareness on something about them that you like, whether it is their coat, or their hair, or the way they gave [up] their seat on the busy bus. Whatever it is that you like, just feel what it feels like in you to meet with your awareness something likable about them.

Now for the hardest one. Picture someone you really do not like. Can you imagine one thing about them that is nice, a gesture, a word? If you find it difficult, imagine them as a child smiling at their mother, or another simple human quality that you do not usually see. Again, try to feel this quality, this meeting of the part of them that is Health.

Now try the same process with a living animal or plant. Tune into something you love about it and allow yourself to focus on how that makes you feel.

Now practice the 'Loving Kindness' technique I talked about earlier.

Start with yourself: **May I be happy; May I be well.**

Then repeat the process for, first, a loved one, then someone you barely know, and finally someone that really annoys you.

May you be happy, may you be well...

May they be happy, may they be well...

Chapter 31

Healing Others

Before we start to discuss this subject, it is important to make totally clear that any so-called 'healing' technique - including this one - must never be used instead of clear medical advice from your doctor or health professional. These techniques are to aid wellbeing and support and should only be used alongside whichever medical treatment is being undertaken.

There are certain important pre-cursors to the practice of healing another, be they a person, or an animal or a plant. The first is that you *show respect* for them. To do this, we must first practice 'Meeting the Health in Others' which we learnt in the last chapter.

The second important process is to *ask permission*. I know it sounds crazy, but we must ask permission to heal another, even if they cannot talk back, like a baby, or a plant or an animal. In these cases, we silently ask permission and wait to see if we can sense a positive response. In the case of another person, we can ask for their permission.

What we are going to do is totally safe if we keep to certain specific rules, which I will go into in detail later. Also, for our purposes, we are going to touch another living thing. This must be done with utmost respect and love and in a manner that is safe to the other person - and ourselves for that matter.

The reason I am teaching you this technique is that I feel everyone on this planet can heal another, we just do not know how to do it. Imagine if everybody knew how to do this. It would be a wonderful thing, and I'm sure would eventually cut down unnecessary visits to the doctor.

Firstly, it is important to state that we cannot heal everything, there are many conditions which healing will not touch. Even in those cases, though, it may bring a little comfort to another and maybe even a softening of their symptoms for a short while. Healing here does not mean a resolution of the problems affecting another person, but if we can harness the innate forces of health within that person's body then it is certainly worthwhile.

At the beginning, it is important to try this on a healthy person. Once you get proficient it will be possible to try this with someone who is unwell.

The next point to make is that there is a perfect meeting place where you and the other person will meet through your gentle, transparent touch. The idea of being transparent here is vital for the technique. Transparent means that you put your hands onto another person in the most gentle way, as if you were touching a newborn baby. The feeling is that you do not want to disturb them. If you imagine that the skin of the person is a delicate fluid, like a very calm sea. You put your hands in place so as not to even make a ripple on the perfect calmness, you have no intention in your hands, they are not actually going to 'do' anything, just rest on this tranquil sea of skin. If you 'meet' the person correctly, with utmost respect it will set up a better healing process.

To meet the Health in another, we must first be able to meet the Health in ourselves, otherwise it will not work as effectively. To do this, before we even touch another, we must set ourselves [up] correctly as we have done in the previous chapter's Practices.

We are also going to use another sense here, the feeling of touch. It is much more than just touch, though, it is using a felt–sense of something deeper, so that we can learn to feel a gentle fluidity in another person. At first you may think this is difficult, but you have already used this same sensory awareness by feeling this within yourself. Even though we are going to use our hands to feel here, we are sensing fluidity with more than just touch. It is more of what I call a felt-sense, which I have mentioned before, which uses touch, proprioception and other subtler sensory apparatus and which we all have.

Imagine you are driving down a bumpy road. How do you know it is bumpy? You are not touching the road at all, you are sensing the bumpiness through the car, the suspension, the wheels and the tyres. This sense is called proprioception and we all use it all the time. This sense is part of what we will use to feel this fluidity in another.

We are also going to feel for certain things and processes, both under our hands and in the whole of the person. We are going to feel for fluidity, expression, softening, [and an] opening quality. We are also going to feel for stillness in the patient and maybe even [feel] the Tide meeting the patient. All these things are possible if we are open to feeling them. Again, with this practice, it is a case of practice making perfect. We are going to apply these processes first to some part of the person that feels good, then we will revisit the technique with some part of the person that is sore or stiff or feels blocked, which takes much more focus and precision.

At the beginning I feel it is important to follow each step, as each step sets up the process perfectly and ensures a positive experience for both you and the person you are trying this on.

Practice 31

Healing Others

I am going to set this out as a sequence of clear steps to follow in order. This ensures effectiveness and a positive experience for everyone involved!

1. *Firstly, choose the other person you want to try this on. Ask permission.*
2. *Get the person to either sit comfortably or lie down on a couch or bed*
3. *Sit yourself in a comfortable position so that you can apply your hands in a way that is comfortable and gentle for both you and them. The general rule is that if you are comfortable then they will be. Play with this - it is probably best to do this first on a finger, or an arm or a leg, or their tummy. What is important here is to find a place in them that is healthy.*
4. *When you have tested for an optimally comfortable position. If you can rest your elbow on the couch all*

the better. This means you can rest your hands on the person without getting tired. You must maintain the softest contact for quite a few minutes.

5. *When you are both comfortably set up in position, let the person rest. Come back to your sitting position without touching them at all.*

6. *We need you to be in a neutral place, so close your eyes, tune into the softness of your breath, like we have done before. Now accept and allow any thoughts, feelings and emotions, all the while bringing back your awareness back to the softness of your breath. As things start to get quiet, allow your awareness to drift to the Stillness that lies behind everything. From here, tune into some part of you that feels soft, fluid and light and just watch that expand a little. All the while, your nervous system is quietening.*

7. *Open your eyes and bring your attention to the person you are going to engage with. Do not touch them yet but let your mind focus on something you like about them, some element of them that is lovely- whatever it is. Really feel how focusing on that makes you feel.*

8. *Now you are ready to apply your relaxed, calm and gentle hands to their arm or leg. If you imagine that their skin is a perfectly calm sea, you are going to rest your transparent hands on this sea of tranquility so as not to disturb [it], not even a ripple.*

9. *When you are comfortable, open your awareness to this calm sea of skin. Get a sense of the depth of it. This whole leg or arm is fluid, and gently breathing at a slow, rhythmic rate. Open your awareness to*

something below your hands that feels, soft, fluid and delicate and that has the quality of lightness to it.

10. Keep your awareness on this delicate, breathing fluidity and watch it grow, becoming beautifully fluid, all the while quietening, softening and with a sense of opening and expanding. Just watch this natural process happen. You are doing nothing at all with your hands, [you are] just watching this process happen.

11. From here, everything starts to get very quiet. The fluids quieten, and you will start to get a sense of Stillness from within the tissues. It feels good. Just watch this deepen - the room can get quiet too.

    This process can take a few minutes. Just let it happen. As the Stillness develops keep part of your attention on the outer room. You may experience the tide coming in.

12. After a while, everything returns to a normal state of quiet fluid breathing. This is the end point of the treatment process.

There are important points to remember here which will be more important when we try this again with tissue that feels blocked, stiff or strained. We need to focus purely on what feels soft, fluid , delicate and healthy.

Let's try this again and this time with some part of the other person that feels a little blocked or unhappy.

Repeat all the steps as before but when you put apply your transparent hands to the tissue and start to sense a degree of fluidity. It is vital not to ignore the blocked, un-fluid feeling that will strike you. Often, it will feel that there is *no delicate, light, fluid part in the blockage. You must search for it. It could be the tiniest speck of fluidity, but when you find it, keep all your attention there and wait until it slowly opens, breathes and expands and the surrounding area becomes more and more fluid. This change in tissue can feel quite strong and striking when you get good at this. The point though is to stay absolutely focused on the fluid expression of Health, no matter how small, and it will grow.*

As you start to get good at finding the Health in the blockage, you will find that you can start to be of quiet help to people. Just by allowing things to soften and 'breathe' a little, you may bring them a little relief.

The more you do this the better you get. I have been doing something quite similar for most days for twenty-five years and I am still learning how to perfect it. But the principle remains the same.

An interesting side-effect of this is that you, as the practitioner, will also feel great afterwards. By focusing on the health and stillness in the patient it naturally brings your body into a balance. Everyone benefits!

I have broken down this process into several steps, but once you are familiar with the principle you will find it surprisingly easy to do.

Try this on your pet, or on a plant in the garden. The same principle applies - and you will be amazed at the result!

Remember, though, this gentle process is not [to be used] instead of proper medical care. It is just a little quiet support and it can feel good for the person you are applying it to.

Chapter 32
Wholeness Meeting
Oneness

There is an underlying process that quietly proliferates as we develop our practice. As we connect more with our own fluid body, as we become more neutral to ourselves, as we get a deepening connection and 'felt- sense' to the Stillness that is all around us and within us, and as we develop a deeper connection to the tide, something starts to happen to us. When we feel our fluid body as a single drop of fluid breathing, in connection to an outer Stillness or the gentle motion of the Tide, we start to feel a sense of wholeness.

Wholeness is defined as 'the state of forming a complete and harmonious whole, a unity.' This is what we can start to feel within us as we practice more and more. We give birth to a sense of self-acceptance that harmonizes us. We feel a sense of wholeness, like we are complete. This brings with it a sense of peace and harmony that grows.

Our bodies start to feel more fluid. This brings with it a feeling of Health and wellbeing. This seems to start to change our own feeling of how the body feels. We become attuned to feelings of fluid, vital healthfulness, and start to enjoy this deepening connection.

What does it mean to feel whole? For me, it involves a deep sense of self-acceptance. We may not be perfect or be 100% Healthy, but we accept all the different parts of us. Our self-judgment softens along with the increasing fluidity we are feeling.

In the process of self-acceptance something else happens. We start to accept and feel a deepening connection with others and the natural world around us. We get a palpable experience of the Stillness and the Tide that connects us all, and through that connection we feel part of a whole, a connected whole. With that, we feel an Oneness - a deep connection - to a wider or greater whole. From the wholeness, a natural consequence is to start to feel part of a greater wholeness, part of nature and part of others. With this brings a natural sense of deepening respect for nature around us and other people and a sense of responsibility for it.

For me this is one of the most important side effects of engaging in a health giving practice. Through deepening connection - and hence respect and responsibility - it becomes harder to be blind to the effect we have on our surroundings. I hope this means that we walk more softly on the earth, that do not disturb it and that we have more responsibility for the nature around us.

From our practice, we can begin to heal ourselves, and others and even support the nature around us. From our developing sensory awareness, we start to sense things we never thought possible and to take notice of the detail in nature we have missed in the past.

We slow our natural tempo to one that is more naturally in sync with nature. This brings further connection and more feelings of oneness with it. As you see, we are not just *thinking* thoughts of Wholeness and Oneness, we are feeling them. This brings them alive and makes them real to us. This goes beyond a simple concept and gives us a sense experience. It takes us from a belief into a reality that we can experience at will.

Practice 32

Wholeness meets Oneness

Let us develop our practice to get a felt-sense of Wholeness and Oneness.

Start as usual by sitting in comfort and tuning into breathing, accepting, allowing and observing everything that arises in the moment.

As everything quietens a little, just bring your awareness to the underlying Stillness behind all noise, the Stillness from which everything begins. All motion begins as stillness, as all life begins in stillness, as everything manifest begins in the un-manifest.

Feel this Stillness and let it build.

Bring your attention now to your body. Feel something that feels fluid. No matter how small, follow the fluid, the delicate expression of fluid Health within your body. Let this fluidity expand and open, so that a bigger and bigger area of your body starts to feel fluid.

Now expand your light attention to your whole body. It is like opening your vision to a wider view.

Sense your body as a complete fluid body, slowly and gently breathing, integrating the parts and connecting up, softening and calming and becoming one. Continue as it starts to feel like a single fluid drop with no boundary, no anatomy, just a single fluid drop, breathing slowly with primary respiration.

Bringing your attention to the horizon now, get a sense of the Stillness that lies there. Get a sense of the Stillness that is everywhere, holding and connecting us all. We are one drop within a sea, all calm and quiet. From the quiet comes the slow Great Tide, breathing us and then returning to the Stillness so very slowly. Our wholeness meeting a greater wholeness, becoming an Oneness.

Chapter 33

Soul Works

The Greek philosopher Plato was the first to discuss the idea of having a Soul. He believed in a dualistic viewpoint of the Body and the Soul/Mind. He believed that the Soul was eternal while the body lasted only for one's life. He believed that there is more to life than what we are usually aware of. His pupil Aristotle refuted this thinking, stating that the soul is more like the life force of the body and that it is not immortal.

Plato's ideas were further explored by the wonderful writings of Italian Renaissance philosopher Marsillio Ficino. Ficino was instrumental in influencing the Renaissance Art Movement, which included the great artists Leonardo Da Vinci and Michelangelo.

Plato also coined the term "aliveness' meaning, for him, deepening a connection to one's soul. His philosophy of medicine looked at the connection of our interior and exterior worlds - our microcosm (inner body) reflecting the outer macrocosm (the nature around us). He looked to music, philosophy and art to explore the inner soul. What we need, he said, is soul, in the middle, holding the mind and body. The soul was a means of connecting ideas and life, connecting the world and the spirit.

Our modern-day view of the soul is slightly wider. It is defined as the spiritual part of humans, or the moralistic. It is also defined as the seat of feelings and sentiment. It is also seen as an animating principle, or a high mindedness, linked with noble and warm feelings, showing spirit or courage. It is also seen as one's essence, or core. Showing soul means to show depth.

In a modern context, two thinkers who have expanded my view of what constitutes Soul are Thomas Moore and John O'Donohue.

Thomas Moore wrote eloquently on 'Care of the Soul', while O' Donohue wrote Anam Cara (Irish), meaning 'soul friend'.

Both authors talked about the depth of Soul work, taking their lead from Ficino and bringing it into modern context. For both writers, Soul is about genuineness and depth, friends and experiences that touch the heart deeply. It is about cultivating a real and honest relationship to ourselves and others. For them, it involves intimate love, both community and aloneness, communion with oneself and the divine elements of life.

Moore, a psychologist by training refuted Soul as a psychology. He defined it more as a deep acceptance of ourselves that is built on honesty. He also saw Soul as an opening up of ourselves to life, to the real experience of living in the moment, whatever pain or beauty that involves.

This is an important part of our practice that we started early on in our techniques. By learning to accept that we have feelings, thoughts and emotions, then to actively allow ourselves to feel them and eventually to Observe the motions of these thoughts, and feelings we are experiencing Soul. With this technique we start on a path of self-acceptance, but to progress I feel we need to engage in some Soul works.

In my view, Soul works embody a slow, gentle view of ourselves, of nature and our community, as well as a deep acceptance of others, which comes first from self-acceptance.

There is something slow about soul works, something about an understanding of depth and a real knowledge that there are elements in our makeup that can be hard to see or live with. There is also an understanding that it is alright to be sad, that it is fine to cry, to be angry or scared, but in all those moments we must be fully alive to them and present to them and accept them as ok. This is hard and slow work, painful in places but affording great joy in others. It is the feeling that it is all ok.

It reminds me of a treatment I gave a few years ago. A lady came to see me, we exchanged only a few words of case history as I intuited she didn't want to talk. I got her to lie down. I started to treat her in exactly the way I have shown you. I was not interested or engaged with specific anatomic or physiological processes. As soon as I put my hands onto her shoulders, she started to sob. She cried for the next twenty minutes as I watched her body relax and release tension. Towards the end, she quietened and her body - and the room - went Still. As the Still-point subsided, she slowly got up, thanked me and left. She never said a word to me about what was troubling her. The process moved me greatly due to its simplicity and depth.

Sometimes it is good to talk, sometimes it works better not to. Both are valid and valuable experiences, and both are Soul work.

The important fulcrum for Soul work for me is honesty and acceptance, both of ourselves, and others. Those actions access our soul, that deep part of us that just wants to be heard, or to communicate silently with us. Art and music connect me with that deeper soul experience and quiet chat with my loved ones helps me feel my Soul.

We each have a way to connect. Often, we forget as we are driven on by the ups and downs of daily life. Sometimes it is easier to connect with your Soul through connection and community, other times it is through solitude and contemplation. It is often different and feels 'Alive', the Aliveness of Plato.

Practice 33

Soul Works

Every day we should give twenty minutes to Soul work, whatever that means for you. I think it important to explore this idea of Soul Work, always bringing in the principles of slowness, allowing time to feel how we feel, deep acceptance of whatever we feel, and deep communication with ourselves or others.

Often that deep communication can go something like this. 'I am feeling sad, alone and tired'. To which I could say "That is fine, Ian, let's rest and listen to some sweet song and eat some fine food or call someone close." The key is first to let yourself feel, then choose something soothing to your soul to nurture yourself with.

Our practice today is to explore the idea of what "soul works" means to you and apply it. Make sure it is slow, accepting and nurturing.

I wish you well in your soul work.

Chapter 34

Re-patterning Our Senses:

Developing a Felt-Sense

As I talked about in the chapter on senses, our five senses develop quite early *in utero*. Our senses of smell, touch and hearing are quite developed by thirty weeks' gestation. From this stage onwards, we are patterning our senses by creating connections between senses, emotions and feelings. For example, the first sounds we hear are the muffled sounds of our mother's voice and heartbeat. These sound rhythms connect us deeply with a sense of nurture and support.

Our early sense of touch is formed by touching our own face and body. It is also formed by our contact with our mother and the feeling of being held in a warm, protective sea of amniotic fluid. We are naked within this sea, so the touch sensors in our whole body become used to this nurturing warm fluid as it holds us safely.

With taste and smell, once again the first thing we sense is our mother, through the amniotic fluid, breast milk and the mother's smell. These imbue, again, a deep sense of connection and nurture. From birth onwards, we are bombarded through our senses. A newborn baby sees without precision, but the brain quickly wires up and can see very acutely from just six months of age.

Our senses from early on are not wired to the higher, more conscious parts of the brain. They are first connected to the brain stem, the preconscious vegetative part of the brain.

Our senses are designed from the beginning to detect simple elements that we need for basic survival. In simple terms, our senses connect us with the external environment. We need to detect the basic idea of whether there is threat or nurture in the surrounding environment and we can then respond reflexively to either.

As a baby if we stroke the outer lip on one side, the baby will move towards the stimulus. This is what is called a primitive reflex and we need it to find food, particularly for finding breast milk from the mother. Other primitive reflexes are designed to reflexively withdraw us from threatening stimuli.

The way the nervous system has been shown to develop is that once the basic instincts for survival are dealt with, such as threat or nurture, we can then go on to develop our social brains. Our social brains enable us to communicate and show emotion, through smiling and other social gestures.

The importance of our senses in this developing story of our nervous systems plays an important but subtle role in the way we use our senses as adults. From early on, we are inundated by a myriad of sense impressions. Just look in front of you right now: how many things can you see without even moving your eyes? Hundreds? Thousands? So, early on, we learn to screen out what is not vital. But how do we perceive what is vital? We are wired to focus primarily on threat and nurture. Later, from adolescence on, another primitive drive enters the fray - that of procreation. We are instinctually driven to turn our senses towards finding potential sexual partners.

As we develop consciousness, our thinking brain - the front of the brain, including the frontal lobes and the emotional regulating limbic parts of the brain - we apply a certain discernment in the way that we apply our senses. But the early experiences that have shaped us leave a silent imprint and pre-consciously guide our attention. Because as we grow and develop, it is only what we put our attention onto that we sense. We screen out most of the elements taken in by our senses.

This sensory awareness also gets shaped early on by the structure of our brain and the proximity of each sense to differing parts of our brain. For example, our olfactory centres of smell in the brain are closely linked to the limbic emotional and memory parts of the brain. Smells can readily bring back emotions and distant memories, but, [in the brain they] are far from language areas, so we find it hard to describe smells.

Our visual and hearing centres are much closer to the language parts of the brain, so we find it much easier to describe sounds and visual stimulus. As we grow, we build up a complex, highly discerning sensory memory. This memory is linked to all these factors I have spoken about – early sense of touch and smell, the development of our social brains and the complex use of sight. It is also from our conscious beliefs and emotions that we connect to each sense experience.

Each distinct sensory experience we have, we categorize in many conscious and unconscious ways. Unconsciously, we are always screening out threats from nurture. Other instinctual drives - like sexual attraction - complicate the process. Consciously, we are always judging everything we see, hear, smell, taste and touch. From simple judgement (do we like it or not?) - to - does this help whatever situation we are needing to engage with, or not?

Each thing that we see, hear, smell, taste or touch goes through multiple layers of screening. Most of them are discarded by preconscious parts of the brain so they are not even sensed. It takes quite a lot of stimuli to provoke a conscious reaction to something that we sense. That is why advertising really tries to grab our attention.

When we lived in ancient times in a degree of harmony with nature it took quite a bit to grab our attention. Man didn't really see every tree, every rock or scrub, only the ones that were deemed important were seen. But now the situation is far worse. The sensory stimulation is totally overwhelming if we do not apply very strong filters. But this in turn makes us insensitive to our environment.

An important question for us here is: are our five senses all we use to sense the world around us or is there more to it?

If we look at the beginnings of life, we start with a fertilized egg, which starts reproducing a few cells. After about a week, these cells form a plate of two layers. By week three of life, a third layer of cells threads between the two layers. These three layers of cells fold to form first a groove and then a tube. This tube is the tube of the brain.

What is interesting here is that the *endoderm* - the inner layer of cells - also becomes the **outer** layer because of the folding. This means that the innermost and the outermost layers of the germ cells are made of the *same material*. These layers go on to develop into the nervous system, including the brain and spinal cord, and the skin. This means that the skin and the brain come from the same place. That is very interesting when we think that our nervous systems are there to interpret and react to sensory input from the environment, and we engage directly with the environment via our skin.

Each cell in our body has its own skin, called its *membrane*. The new sciences of Cell Biology and Epigenetics have shown that our development is less controlled by our genes than the environment around them. The cell membrane is highly sensory. It is sensitive and reactive to the environments around it. The cell membrane reacts within the cell to switch genes on and off.

Scientific thinking is changing its view from a genetics bias to that of the environment being the key to development. If we take this point of view, we can see that every cell in our body has layers and layers of receptors. These receptors are influenced by many things in the surrounding environment, from subtle fluid changes, electromagnetic changes to biochemical changes. You could say that each cell in our body has a sensory awareness. If you think of the billions of cells we are made of and how they function together, we can start to see that our whole body is a sensory apparatus. We are totally sensory!

Consider the growing science behind the idea that our heart acts more than just a pump. We all have a feeling that our hearts have a greater role, especially in emotion. We have all felt heartache. It is a real sense coming from our chest and it is emotional. There is increasing evidence that is corroborated by our own sensory experience that our heart is also a sensory organ. In that we can feel and connect through our heart with the world and with other people. When we look at all of this together we must look at our senses as much more than our five sensory organs.

We started to explore these themes in earlier chapters, but here we want to really develop our sensory experience, so we are far more conscious of its full potential.

The idea of a 'Felt-Sense' expands our usual view of our senses. This sense is not made up of any particular sense but includes an ever-changing combination of senses. Much more than that, though, through it we can learn to sense throughout the entirety of our systems, like we are one huge cell membrane which, can sense the environment on multiple levels at the same time.

This idea of a multi-level sensory awareness is very much helped by the feeling of fluidity. If we sense the world through our Fluid body, we become totally sensory. All our individual senses connect to allow us to have overall impressions, which are felt within a fluid field. It is like we are a fluid field, which is purely sensory, engaging with the world around, which is also fluid and sensory. Maybe this is due to our earliest sensing of the world being entirely fluid within the amniotic fluid.

If we can become skilled at engaging with the world via this fluid field, the result can be that our senses begin to re-pattern, renew and refresh, to lose their learnt biases and become open to sensing the beauty of the world around us. We *literally* start to sense the world around us differently.

Practice 34

Felt Sense

Felt – Sense is the opposite to our thinking, analytical way that many of us are used to of seeing the world. It is about sensing without judgment and being open to experience the world through our developing sensory awareness.

For this our mind must be neutral, so we minimalize any mental projections of what we are sensing, whether in nature or ourselves.

Let us start by sitting quietly and by sensing a degree of Stillness that is always present behind everything.

We are sensing this underlying Stillness with what I call Felt-Sense. We cannot hear or see the Stillness, but we can feel it. This sensory apparatus we are using employs our senses. It is more than any sense by itself and more than all five senses combined. We are feeling something with our whole being.

It helps if we are attuned to our fluid body. First sense first a degree of fluidity somewhere within your body, and allow accept and observe any thoughts, feelings and emotions that arise as we have done many times by now in our previous practices.

Once you find some fluidity, allow this to expand. Slowly you will feel yourself becoming totally fluid, a fluid body slowly breathing. This entirely sensory fluid body we experience can be used to sense our surroundings.

Keep an awareness of your Fluid body as you sense this Stillness all around you and let that perception deepen naturally.

As before, allow your Felt-Sense to breathe out to the horizon and wait until you feel the Great Tide - a motion coming from Stillness as it slowly breathes you, moves through you as a Great Tide moving you, holding you and connecting you to life.

Allow your Felt-Sense to expand and try to sense something in your environment, be it a plant, flower or person. Do not touch them but allow this Felt-Sense from your fluidity to meet and sense the fluidity of the chosen person or thing. Can you feel it? Without using touch in the usual way, we can start to feel or sense our surroundings.

This is your Felt-Sense and it will connect you. It will also expand and deepen your sensory experience. Are you becoming more aware that we have a much deeper ability within our sensory apparatus than we use in daily life?

Chapter 35

Sensing Wholeness in Nature

'Look deeply into nature and you will understand everything better'.
Albert Einstein

In an earlier chapter, we started to explore the history of the development of our thinking about the world - from philosophy to science - and how we have strived to understand ourselves, and nature.

Certain approaches to thinking have informed how we see the world and these have become so engrained in our world-view that we are simply unaware that we are affected by them.

Ever since René Descartes introduced the idea by saying 'I think therefore I am.' He introduced the concept of dualism, meaning the process of thinking being key to our understanding of the world.

Through this Cartesian approach, we see nature as separate to ourselves. The subject (us) and the object (nature) become two separate entities and through the process of *thought* we learn to understand nature.

A materialistic approach to Science has been borne out of this dualistic concept. Science has sought to understand nature by quantifying and measuring it. This process of analysis breaks down nature into its components, then tries to put these elements together to understand the whole. Unfortunately, this [analysis? Concept? Problem – if so, what is the problem?] is compounded by the idea that there are many ways of seeing the same thing. For example, the idea that the world was flat, stationary and at the centre of the universe makes a good deal of sense if we use our senses in a normal way. How could the earth be moving through space at great speed and still feel stable?

Copernicus turned the world upside-down by stating that the earth is moving, as are all the planets, around the sun. He had no evidence of this at the time, but he employed a jump in understanding in stating that 'if the earth is moving, we in fact will be moving with it so would not feel the motion'.

But in many ways, science has not until recently thought past this Cartesian dualistic thinking. One person who thought beyond this was Johann Wolfgang Goethe (1749-1832). Goethe was principally known as a poet and philosopher based in Germany. During a trip to Italy in 1788, he became fascinated with the wealth of flowers and plants he saw in the countryside there and with Renaissance painting. Subsequently, he spent twenty years researching colours, optics and the biology of plants.

He discovered in his journey – and about 150 years before it was explored again - the idea that scientific knowledge is intrinsically historical, as opposed to factual. Scientific discovery was bound by the preconceptions of the scientists involved - and their education and cultural history - thereby implying that science changes because our ways of seeing change.

Goethe started to look at nature from a different perspective. He looked at the inherent Wholeness of nature and perceived the whole deeply. He also developed the idea that to observe nature deeply, one becomes a participant in the process. This truly holistic approach removes the dualistic Cartesian concept of a subject being separate from an object. It reconnects them. He looked deeply at the flowering plants and perceived that the plant was not made up of constituent parts but of a wholeness that becomes each part.

This idea is like that of the *hologram*. The hologram is a photographic plate produced by a particularly sharp laser, which holds light together without it dispersing. What is amazing about the Hologram is that if you take a small pixel of a normal photo or picture you see just one part of the whole. In a hologram, each pixel contains an image of the whole. In a normal picture, if you take away some of its parts, you will lose the coherence of the picture. With a hologram, though, if you take away some parts you retain the image but just a little bit more dispersed. The Hologram is a nice example of Wholeness because each part contains the whole.

Goethe expanded this thinking to the idea of *morphology*, a term he coined to look at the inherent shapes in plants and animals. He used the term differently to how we use it today. He would sense a plant or animal, looking deeply [into its nature]. His holistic vision could be termed intuitive (meaning looking deeply). I think he employed what we have called a Felt-Sense and reached an understanding of the inherent Wholeness of the plant or animal and from it could *see* all other plants within it. Here, Wholeness meets Oneness in a sensory way.

This is an interesting idea to try out practically. As soon as we try to apply rational, analytic language, we are using a different part of our brain. We quickly lose the inherent ability to sense this Wholeness and Oneness. An example of this is this: whilst listening to birdsong this morning, my partner said, "I wish that I could understand what they are saying." I got her to try a little *holistic listening*, asking her to employ her Felt-Sense at the same time.

The process went as follows: We started to sense the birdsong as a whole. This involves softening our hearing a little to hear the many birds who are singing as one holistic entity.

"But what am I supposed to hear?" she asked. My response was that there is no *supposed* about it. If we suppose anything we are bringing in our analytic mind. "Let's feel the birdsong as a *whole*, as a unity within which are all the different birds," I answered. This was easier to understand and soon we both could feel the birdsong as a whole.

Then I asked her, "try to feel, not hear, what they are saying within the Wholeness. Do not employ language or try to apply a language to what you feel or hear." This was possible and so, without putting words to it, we could sense what the birds were saying but not within our human language.

Approaching the birdsong in that way brought us into a deep sense of connection with the birds and the birdsong. The idea that observer and observed become part of the phenomenon being observed is something that we start to sense. This may sound strange but, in the Practice, we will try it and I hope you get a sensory impression of it.

The old Daoist wizards would employ similar practices to the above to achieve a variety of effects. There are great stories told in many books, of the old wise men employing their sensory skills and intention to change local weather patterns or connect deeply with plants and animals. With weather patterns it is fascinating to try to employ our Felt-Sense of wholeness, (which I will call holistic Felt-Sense) to sense for example, a wind or rain pattern. When you do this try to sense the whole weather pattern, sense the whole thing without analyzing it and see what it feels like. When we start to sense these natural elements as a whole it can leave a very different sensory impression.

I personally like to try to sense the sun and its energy as a whole as I do a standing practice in the mornings. It seems to connect me more to it and feels wonderful to do.

Throughout history there have been stories of shamans or healers from many indigenous cultures who learnt to connect their energy with that of certain elements in nature. They used their connection with nature to heal others. The process would seem to involve a sharpened and expanded sensory awareness.

About 15 years ago I started to teach a course for osteopaths called *Developing Palpation*. I have always considered that the more precisely that we can feel things, the more effective our practice becomes. One of the Practices we would do was a re-thinking of anatomy. At undergraduate level of study, the students learnt anatomy from dissection and anatomy books to a very high level of detail. This would prove a problem when trying to feel or palpate living anatomy. This is because the students by this time had developed a high level of analytic thinking. When trying to feel anatomy and physiology, they would impose on the tissue what they *thought* the anatomy would feel like.

Dissection is carried out with relatively dry tissue, not fluid, living tissue. [When pictures are used], they are nothing like living tissue. It was even harder for them as I was asking them to feel and sense living tissue inside the body using their hands from the outside.

The practice would involve a certain amount of trying to let go of their learning and to work with Felt-Sense. [To help them] to gain sensory impressions of what they felt, I allowed them to open out their language so as not to slip back into the analytic mind again. They would use colour, tone, texture and whatever other language they could find to help find a new sensory understanding of what they were feeling. The added dimension of developing a sensory impression of the Wholeness of whatever we are engaging with adds a deeper dimension to our practice.

This idea of holistic Felt-Sense can open a whole new way of engaging with the world. By learning to sense nature holistically, we can deepen our connection to it and gain some amazing insights from it.

This can make us *holistic scientists of nature* by sensing natural processes deeply to gain a richer understanding of ourselves, and nature.

It is interesting that the scientific works of Goethe were discounted at the time when Newtonian analytical views of science were preferred. In recent times, especially through some of the findings from modern physics - where the idea that the observer has a measurable effect on the observed - that this thinking has started to change.

Since the 1960s, science has understood more of the idea that a scientific viewpoint will vary due to there being different ways of seeing the same phenomena.

Recently, the scientific philosophy of Goethe has begun to be reviewed. More interest has been shown in the idea of looking at phenomena in nature holistically, deeply observing as a whole - not as a way of replacing analytic science, but as another method of looking into nature to understand it better.

The English poet and painter William Blake (1757-1827) lived at the same time as Goethe. I do not know if they knew each other's work, but I see a great affinity between the two.

In his poem *Auguries of Innocence*, Blake says:

'To see the world in a grain of sand

And heaven in a wild flower

Hold infinity in the palm of your hand

And eternity in an hour'.

These words for me echo the act of observing Wholeness, which Goethe employed and explains it beautifully. They have a deep meaning and open to us a world of possibilities when we allow ourselves to sense the world deeply and in Wholeness.

Let's try now to work a little with this holistic Felt-Sense.

Practice 35

Holistic Felt-Sense

At this stage in our practice, we should be familiar and becoming proficient at a variety of practices. We can bring our mind to a quite neutral, where we allow, accept and finally just observe our thoughts, feelings and emotions. We can bring our awareness to the present moment, feel our fluid body and sense Stillness in and around us. From the Stillness, we can sense the motion of the Great Tide as it slowly breathes through nature. We have started to develop our sensory awareness, and re-pattern our senses, and in doing so have started to develop a Felt-Sense where we can expand our sensory awareness to feel nature around us.

For this practice, we will take things a little further away from our analytic mind, to our open sensory field of awareness. In so doing, we open ourselves to new and beautiful impressions of nature.

Let's start with sitting quietly – ideally outside in a garden or in nature in some way. It doesn't matter if it is nighttime or daytime.

Bring your mind to a quiet neutral in the way we have done so many times by now, allowing everything and bringing attention slowly back to the softness in your breath.

Allow your attention to rest on the great Stillness that is everywhere, and behind everything.

Now choose something in nature to observe or listen to, it doesn't matter what. Let's say, for example, we are listening to birdsong, or looking at a flower, or feeling wind on our cheek. It is not important what primary sense you use. I will use the birdsong example.

*Listen to the song, then try to listen to all the birds singing together. Allow your mind to sense them all as a unified whole, which is **birdsong**. From here let your felt–sense meet this wholeness of birdsong and try to **feel it**. Feeling it has a wonderful effect of connecting you deeply to the birdsong, doesn't it? It is almost as if you become part of the unified birdsong.*

*For me there are two elements to this sensing. The first is depth - we are sensing deeply, as if penetrating the superficial to sense a deeper story within the whole. The second is breadth - taking in the whole. This is not an overview but an opening of our awareness to the whole. Now without employing your analytic mind or giving words or language, see if you can **feel** what the birds are saying. This is language beyond words, bird language - can you **feel** their communication? It is wonderful, isn't it?*

Chapter 36

Living on the Tide

(Beyond Technique)

In this concluding chapter, I will recap the practices and processes we have been developing and developed our awareness of.

This book is based on a course I have been teaching for over 10 years. The course is Practice and sensory. It has been interesting to format into a book. It has allowed me to explain how my approach has developed in more detail.

We have been on a journey of discovery. The journey started with simple basic processes and, by the end, we have looked at complex sensory practices. On our journey, we have learned many techniques and practices, each of which builds on the perceptual understanding of the last. Without the foundational practices, the latter stages are impossible. Learning here involves a sensory change – literally, a change in perception and even consciousness. Then, changes become embodied and they have a lasting effect.

We started with learning about the idea of Neutral, the process of taking our minds out of gear so that our being can return to a more childlike state, not driven ever forwards by our will. To actively achieve this, it immediately brought us into contact with our thoughts, feelings and emotions. We learnt to actively accept, allow and finally learn to observe [these parts of ourselves] without judgment.

From here we looked at the ideas of **timing** and **tempo**. In the process, we learnt to become aware of a natural timing and flow [of things].

Next, we looked at the importance of **developing a daily practice** and the steps we can take to do so.

This was followed by focusing on our **sitting posture**, to find a good technique and comfort for our sitting practice, whilst still keeping a good posture.

We then looked at the **Gift of the Present**, the process of bringing our awareness and attention into the present moment.

Then we explored the wonderful experience of learning to **sense the great Stillness** that is always present and lies behind all activity. We started to develop a living relationship with this Stillness. We were starting to gain awareness of our **attention**, looking at where it is in time and space. We then looked at the process of giving something our full, clear attention and the benefits of Pure Attention.

From here, we began to become aware of natural **Still-points**, when and where they develop naturally without our volition. Our senses become aware when they arise and naturally enjoy them.

Our practice then developed a little by learning to **settle into Stillness,** employing a combination of techniques to allow ourselves to find and relax into a state of Stillness.

From here, we turned our attention to ourselves and learnt a technique to start to feel **fluidity** within our body and to let that fluidity manifest to eventually feel like we are one fluid body.

Once able to feel this internal fluidity we turned our attention to the **fluid fields** around us, the sense that everything around us and in nature also has fluidity, which, with our growing sensory awareness, can learn to feel like living in a sea of fluidity.

With this new knowledge about fluidity, we looked at some of the great indigenous tribes of the world and the connection they felt with this sea or wind, the **Story on the wind**.

We next studied the idea that within this fluidity there is a motion, a slow breathing fluid motion we could call the **Great Tide** or the **Long Tide**. We went on to practice feeling it, learning to take our awareness to the stillness and waiting until motion arises from Stillness.

Next, we started on an exploration of our **senses**, how we use them and how we have programmed them. The course has been about developing sensory awareness, meaning developing our senses, so first we had to understand a little of how they function.

We then practiced letting our **senses open** and breathe more fully and deeply.

Developing our sensory awareness brought us into a greater sense of **connection** with our surrounds and the wholeness of nature. From here, we looked at some of the Daoist ideas of **flow** and **movement** and how it relates to Stillness.

With each technique we were deepening our sensory understanding of Neutral and Stillness - both inside and outside of ourselves - and of motion - notably when and where it arises from Stillness.

We went on to concentrate our awareness at that place in our sensory field that Motion arises and to keep our attention there and wait to see what happens.

Fulcrums were explored in the next phase. This served the purpose of allowing us to be aware of exactly where our attention lies in each moment.

From here we started to look at the important process of **changing our attention** from what in us feels blocked, unhappy or ill at ease to what feels sweet, light and fluid. This was first looked at by the idea of directing our breath to areas of our body as a soft and releasing breath. This started us on the process of connecting to the **potential for Health within our bodies**.

This was followed up by an exploration of the **Fire of ignition**, the practice of engaging with the animating potency within us.

After this, we briefly explored some Daoist **Standing practices** where we learned to connect our energy with that of certain natural elements, like the earth, the sun, trees and plants.

Next, we started to explore and practice the idea and sense of **Dynamic Stillness**, or Wu Wei, which is the Stillness that contains the potential for all motion. This brought specific sensory changes, which we explored in detail.

We went on to look at **true spontaneity**, or returning to the natural, which involves a slow releasing of conditioned responses to life, so we can live fully and freely within the moment.

Then we picked up the process of **letting Stillness proliferate** or deepen, naturally deepening our practice further.

From here, we developed the ideas of **Meeting our Health** to learn a practice of self-healing, which we then learned to use in the practice of **healing others**.

We then introduced the idea and experience of **Wholeness** and how that potentially meets **Oneness**.

This led on to a discussion of the idea of **Soul** and **Soul-work**, which involves a deepening self-acceptance and awareness.

We then revisited our senses, further exploring them and introducing the concept of **Felt-Sense**, something which combines our sense but is more than our senses as we know them. We also looked at the process of **re-patterning** our senses.

This led us into an exploration of sensing nature and the practice of developing a **Holistic Felt-Sense** and through it how we can gain deep insights into nature.

These processes have, I hope, started to achieve the following in us:

- Deepened self-awareness and self-acceptance and the ability to bring our mind to Neutral.
- Expanded sensory awareness and the development of a Holistic Felt- Sense whilst re-patterning our senses.
- An ever-deepening relationship with Stillness in and around us.
- A relationship with the Great Tides in nature and connection to them.
- A change in perception from looking at disease to seeing Health in ourselves, and others.
- A Practice technique of self-healing and healing others.
- A variety of sitting and standing practices for healing and developing perceptual awareness.
- A developing relationship with Dynamic Stillness or Wu Wei.

All of the above when put together make for a pretty comprehensive practice, which has the potential to be deeply transformative and life-changing.

But what about in normal daily life? What about if you are deeply worried about someone close, or a job situation or finance and feel deeply stressed? Can any of this be helpful if all you can think about is something that is a very real worry? Is it possible, through all this practice, to live in Stillness, connection and Health [regardless]?

The reality, for me, is that through being ill, through deep stress and through life, I have learnt to use these techniques to help me through. Do I get stressed, angry, upset, fearful, insecure, sad?

Absolutely and as much as ever! But when I am [in any of these negative emotional states], I do a little practice and it really does help.

The first point is to practice the accept, allow, observe process and just let the stress BE the stress - it's ok.

Then we can employ one or two of the many techniques we have explored to change our reaction to the stress. It does not remove the stress but helps change the way we react to it.

But how can we practice in everyday life? When I do my daily practice, I do the following first thing each morning:

- I go for a run, stretch a lot then do some standing practice like I showed you earlier.
- Then I come inside and do about 20-40 minutes of sitting practice.

I do not follow a set sequence of practice. It is always a little bit different. If I did the same practice every day, my mind would get used to it, get bored and switch off - and I would probably sleep!

This Dynamics of Stillness practice is a little different from meditation because it involves sensory awareness, felt-sense and allowing our attention to move, either through our own volition or by the Tide or the moment.

My goal [in my daily practice] often changes. It can be to sense nature deeply, feel the Tide, feel Stillness or to do a little self-healing. Whatever I do on any given day, it is all practice.

I use what I call **Ways into Stillness**, which I always change. I start with either softness of breath, or sensing Stillness, or waiting for the Tide, or practicing acceptance and observing whatever I am feeling. What I am attuned to is the developing, proliferating Stillness and eventually to Wu Wei or Dynamic Stillness. If my sensory awareness is focused on [the potential for this developing], I will employ one or two ways [from the practices] - from anything we have covered in this book - but I never use just one. I try to allow my mind to be moved by the moment, to always allow and never to fix it.

When Dynamic Stillness arrives, it brings a state of no–mind, almost an emptiness where I lose time and space for a while. This can last ten minutes or much more. But, eventually, my attention returns. It may become a process of unwinding, or of feeling warmth in my body, or a feeling of the Tide arriving or birdsong or the wind, which I may concentrate on with **holistic felt-sense** for a while.

Often though, I am left with a thought or feeling as to something to write or do. Often, it is something that has resolved itself in my mind without me [actively] thinking about it at all. I trust this sense, as I feel it comes from somewhere deeper in me.

What is nice is to take two things with me into the day:

1. The first is an awareness of the underlying Stillness that is behind everything. If I try to check in with this during the day, then my day feels peaceful and more enjoyable.
2. The other is trying to be aware of a sense of when Motion arises from the Stillness, or a sense of when The Great Tide moves through me. This feels deeply healing and connecting.

This could be what the Daoists call being *with the Dao* or being moved by life. Again, the more I do it, the more I can do it. Practice really makes these perceptual processes come alive.

Throughout the day, I personally like to use my Felt-sense to connect with nature whenever I can – I just really enjoy it. I think we all can develop our own practice that works best for us. Everyone is different, but at this stage it is important to develop your own Way of Practice and make it your own.

I really hope you enjoy these practices. They have been deeply enriching for me, so much so that I wanted to share what I have spent years learning and working with.

I have produced an online course in this subject where I describe some of these processes and take you through a series of practices- check Thedynamicsofstillness.com for details.

Practice 36

Beyond Technique

At this stage, we should be able to practice standing, sitting, whilst on a train or anywhere really. We should be able to do this in nature, alone or even in a crowded room.

We do not at this stage need step-by-step instructions. Instead, let our attention focus on some developing sensations whilst being moved by the moment. Sense stillness and motion.

Start with the process of Allowing Accepting and then Observing all thoughts, feelings and emotions – whether they be good or bad.

At the same time, let your attention fall onto whatever comes up. This could be the Stillness all around us, or a sense of something that feels soft, delicate or fluid in your body, or the feeling of motion of the great Tide as it arises from Stillness.

Try to let your attention be moved by whatever comes up but always let your attention come back to the proliferating Stillness in and around you.

Be aware also of the softening and opening and calming process within you. Allow all this to happen at the same time without fixing your attention.

When your attention softens itself into Dynamic Stillness just go with that process and be taken by it. There is no technique but a deepening Dynamic Stillness.

I wish you well.

Ian

Printed in Great Britain
by Amazon